Richard Nelson

PLAYS TWO

Richard Nelson's plays include *Farewell to the Theatre*, *Nikolai and the Others*, *Sweet and Sad*, *That Hopey Changey Thing*, *Conversations in Tusculum*, *How Shakespeare Won the West*, *Frank's Home*, *Rodney's Wife*, *Franny's Way*, *Madame Melville*, *Goodnight Children Everywhere*, *The General From America*, *New England*, *Misha's Party* (with Alexander Gelman), *Columbus or the Discovery of Japan*, *Two Shakespearean Actors*, *Some Americans Abroad*, *Left*, *Life Sentences* and *Principia Scriptoriae*. He has written the musicals *Unfinished Piece for a Player Piano* (with Peter Golub); *James Joyce's The Dead* (with Shaun Davey), *My Life with Albertine* (with Ricky Ian Gordon); and screenplays for the films *Hyde Park-on-Hudson* (Roger Michell director) and *Ethan Frome* (John Madden director).

He has received numerous awards both in America and abroad, including a Tony Award (Best Book of a Musical for *James Joyce's The Dead*), an Olivier Award (Best Play for *Goodnight Children Everywhere*), Tony nominations (Best Play for *Two Shakespearean Actors*; Best Score as co-lyricist for *James Joyce's The Dead*), an Olivier nomination (Best Comedy for *Some Americans Abroad*), two Obies, a Lortel Award, a New York Drama Critics Circle Award, a Guggenheim Fellowship and a Lila Wallace–Readers' Digest Writers Award. He is recipient of the PEN/Laura Pels Master Playwright Award, an Academy Award from the American Academy of Arts and Letters, and is an Honorary Associate Artist of the Royal Shakespeare Company. He lives in upstate New York.

T0333380

RICHARD NELSON

Plays Two

THREE PLAYS OF ADOLESCENCE

Goodnight Children Everywhere

Franny's Way

Madame Melville

with an introduction
by the author

faber and faber

First published in 2012
by Faber and Faber Limited
74–77 Great Russell Street, London WC1B 3DA

Typeset by Country Setting, Kingsdown, Kent CT14 8ES
Printed in England by CPI Group (UK) Ltd, Croydon CR0 4YY

Goodnight Children Everywhere
first published by Faber and Faber Limited, 1998
Madame Melville
first published by Faber and Faber Limited, 2000
Franny's Way
first published by Broadway Play Publishing, 2003

A CIP record for this book
is available from the British Library

ISBN 978–0–571–28071–1

2 4 6 8 10 9 7 5 3 1

Contents

Introduction

CHILDREN

I stumbled upon this; or perhaps life just presented it.

For a good while, I had been exploring in my plays certain themes: displacement, exile and loss, what one might call a general sense of homelessness or rootlessness. I suspect this is how I see the world, both personally and politically or socially. I have explored these themes in literal ways in plays where characters are in exile or have lost their home. In one, an English family lives spread out across the wide expanse of America, as rootless and lost as any other that finds itself in the purgatory of exile. In another, American academics wander around England's great cultural cathedrals, struggling unsuccessfully to find some connection or meaning in these edifices that might relate to themselves and their lives. And yet another charts the tragedy of America's greatest traitor, which ends in his leaving his home for ever.

There have been quite a few others, also singing these same haunting themes, though perhaps less literally, where characters, though not exactly homeless, are still estranged emotionally, politically, humanly from what had been their home. I wrote these plays often wondering where all these feelings where coming from. And wondering if perhaps I was on to something larger than my own fears, and perhaps even dealing with something quintessentially late-twentieth century or early twenty-first century – a time in which the world gets smaller, even as any sense of home, place, belonging, seems to be ever more out of our reach.

Then my daughters became teenagers; and in them I saw every day in front of me two young women struggling with these same feelings, but in a whole different context or vocabulary: that is, as – adolescents. Here too were the questions of belonging, feelings of loss and confusion, and of a world greater and distant from ourselves; here too fear, anxiety and that sense of being separate from all things. I saw all this in them, but, unlike the exiles I had been writing about, here I found protagonists who approached these fears with a kind of hope (or is it innocence), even with a sense of thrill and daring. Their doubts, questions and fears were just as dangerous and potentially destructive, but they were found now in a world that was alive, ready to be explored.

And as I watched my children grow, I watched not only them, but myself – and myself not only as I am today, but as I was as a child. I assume this is true of any parent. I had thoughts and memories I'd forgotten or repressed or hidden about my own childhood; they all came rushing back. I had heard others say: *as we raise our children, we also relive our lives.* And this is what I was experiencing.

So I stumbled upon the discovery: that my old themes, of exile and loss, had their roots here too – in adolescence, and out of these roots, my themes grew new shoots. Adolescence too – just like political and emotional exile – asks these questions: Where do I belong? Why am I afraid?

I realised there was also something unique about the exile of adolescence. Here the fears aren't directed at anything specific in the world, but instead at something raw and vulnerable in ourselves. And, as such, these fears seemed to express themselves in ways almost primal and mythic and certainly irrational. As a writer I decided to take a leap into this world, as one might jump down the proverbial rabbit hole, or so it has often felt. So down I went. And these three plays are the result of that jump; unlike any of my other plays, these three have this in common – at the centre of each are children or a child.

FAIRY TALES

In some ways, while on this adventure, I did not stray that far from my earlier plays; I had often set my stories in distant lands and distant times; and here again I set these plays in the past and in foreign places. But these plays feel very different to me, and perhaps the 'rabbit hole' image is the best way to describe that difference. The settings and times *are* quite specific, and the worlds *are* realistically presented; however, the stories these characters act out come, I think, from someplace stranger, more unreal and irrational; more out of the world of fairy tales than 'real life'.

Goodnight Children Everywhere

The prodigal son returns, to a world where everything is changed – his three sisters are now women, one even pregnant. When last seen they were children, but now magically, suddenly, they are changed – at least in the brother's eyes. And of course he is magically changed in theirs. The sisters are taken care of by an older unreliable man; parents are gone – vanished, leaving only mysteries, memories and magical traces. These are abandoned children; abandoned now in the woods of a half-destroyed landscape where amazing things happen: a boy is a man is a boy; a brother becomes a father becomes a lover. A girl puts on a dress and becomes her mother. And all ends with the birth of a baby and a comforting, albeit haunting, lullaby.

Franny's Way

Two children wander into a forest, guided by their grandmother; this forest is full of jazz, temptation, excitement, and sexual possibility; it's called Greenwich Village in the fifties. This world entices and beckons, like sirens on the sea. Yet it is also a world of death and sudden inexplicable loss, where sex has become fused with guilt and rage. A healthy, happy baby is suddenly taken away. A child pulls a trick and seeks her lost mother; another nearly seduces her cousin's husband, misunderstanding his pain for attraction. Here is a forest full of dangers and inexplicable seductions and misunderstandings. By the end, the girls escape, unharmed, and again, a child is born to replace the one stolen.

Madame Melville

Here the forest is a truly magical and wondrous place, full of knowledge, and the pleasure of art; all of which is hopelessly and thrillingly entwined with sex. A boy has run away, thrown all caution to the wind; in one magical night he hopes to grow up and understand the world and to feel a part of this brave new world. Of course he learns more than he ever intended or could then understand, and so the mysteries of that night will be revealed to him slowly over time. And all ends, as so often in a fairy tale, when out of the blue arrives a figure, who says nearly nothing – a large and threatening figure – who literally picks up the child and takes him home. The spell of the dream has now been broken. Gone is the Queen of the Night – or was she a witch who bewitched him?

SEX

Sex with your brother; sex with your sister; an innocent game ends with masturbation, guilt and longing; sex with your teacher; a secret rendezvous to have sex with a boyfriend; the hidden diaphragm as talisman; all of this sex threading its way through these worlds full of runaways, abandonment, absent parents, sudden inexplicable deaths (of a child, of a lover, of parents), sudden inexplicable arrivals (of a father, of a suitor). This is the world of childhood, and the memory of childhood: the world of nightmares and dreams and adolescent sexual fantasy.

THE MEMORY OF CHILDHOOD

Two of these plays are memory plays: that is, a narrator remembering his or her past tells them to us. I think both are attempts to explore something I mentioned earlier – that as we watch our children grow, we also watch ourselves, and relive our childhood.

Franny's Way

Franny, now an older woman, tells us a story of the weekend she spent in Greenwich Village when she was seventeen. In the re-enactment of her memory, Franny takes the role of the grandmother who was the chaperon for that weekend, and over the two days was put to many a test. So we see the story from the points of view of the child – what Franny remembers – but told to us from the perspective of the adult, responsible for the children, trying to protect them in the forest, but also to keep alive, or find again, what the adult has lost or buried or hidden.

Madame Melville

Carl, now an older man, tells us the story of his night with his attractive French teacher, Claudie, in Paris in the sixties. However, we never actually see this older Carl, only the boy. It's the boy we see and hear speaking the words of the adult man. In the adult Carl's memory, he can only see himself as a child; the adult has no place here. So we hear the adult, but see the child; perhaps that is how we often remember.

TIME AND PLACE

I think I chose what could be called three archetypal, even mythic, times and places for these three plays – settings that kindle vivid images and memories for many people, and certainly for me.

Goodnight Children Everywhere

I first got the idea for a play set in postwar London when I saw on the London Underground a poster for a museum exhibition. It had an evocative photograph of a young girl, a name tag around her neck, sitting on a suitcase, waiting at a train station. She was waiting to be evacuated from London in the Second World War. Is there another time in British history that has such deep and resonant and unresolved emotional pull? During the play's run in Stratford, at every single performance I attended someone approached me to say that he or she too had been evacuated during the war.

Franny's Way

Salinger's *Franny and Zooey* defined my adolescence (along of course with *The Catcher in the Rye*). The world of Salinger represents to my generation something far greater than the world of literature. Reading his books was the first time when you saw yourself in literature, your self-doubts, your anger, and the discomfort of your own skin. Suddenly art meant something. And it was a moment when you felt – *I am not alone*. Even if we never ventured into the 'beat' world of Greenwich Village, we certainly could imagine what it must be like; and I'm sure many of us did – in our dreams.

Madame Melville

I remember when, at the age of fifteen, I discovered French films: all the obvious ones of the sixties – Truffaut, Godard, Chabrol – as well as others I indiscriminately loved just because they were being shown in an 'art house' cinema. It was the same time I discovered that there was a world called Art. All of this is inseparable now in my memory – France, Paris, sixties, art, foreign films, jazz, and certain books and painters – and all of this kindled a passionate desire to be an artist, and to write. The play is set in 1966, a year on a cusp – when change was everywhere in the air.

These three plays were written over a fairly short period of time, probably two and a half years. Though not conceived together, they grew out of the same impulse, and have one important structural similarity: they are each set in one room. And in each case, this room has doors and, when open, we see through these doors to other rooms, hallways, bedrooms. Worlds exist just beyond our view, just around a corner, in the next room. A young married couple have sex in that next room; a baby dies in another room behind a half-closed door; a brother and sister head to their parents' old bedroom (we see the door down the hall); through another is a kitchen, another the teacher's bedroom. Voices are heard, acts imagined. I think that is central to the emotion of these plays.

The first title for *Madame Melville* was *Incertain*, French for 'uncertain', a title I could have called any of these plays. When writing *Melville*, I kept a newspaper clipping taped to the first page of my notebook; it was from a brief article in *The New York Times* by a Princeton professor, Alexander Nahama: 'Uncertainty – the sense that not only you don't know the truth but that many complex issues are irresolvably ambiguous – is sometimes the most productive way of allowing yourself to act . . . It produces a tentativeness that permits you to see many things from many points of view. Which is, I believe, the best definition of objectivity.'

These three plays have never before been published together.

RN, 2011

Lyrics from 'Goodnight Children Everywhere', written by Harry Phillips and Gaby Rogers, published by Cecil Lennox Ltd., a Kassner Group Company, Exmouth House, 11 Pine Street, London ECIR OJH.

Lyrics from 'The Bells of St. Mary's'. written by A. Emmett Adams and Douglas Furber, published by Chappell & Co. Inc., c/o Warner Chappell Music Inc., 10585 Santa Monica Boulevard, Los Angeles, CA 90025.

Lyrics from 'Hernando's Hideaway', from *The Pajama Game*, written by Richard Adler and Jerry Ross, Lakshmi Puja Music Ltd. and The Songwriters Guild, 1500 Harbor Boulevard. Weehawken, NJ 07087.

GOODNIGHT CHILDREN EVERYWHERE

Goodnight Children Everywhere was first performed by the Royal Shakespeare Company at The Other Place, Stratford-upon-Avon, on 4 December 1997. The cast, in order of appearance, was as follows:

Betty Sara Markland
Ann Cathryn Bradshaw
Vi Robin Weaver
Mike Colin McCormack
Peter Simon Scardifield
Hugh Malcolm Scates
Rose Aislinn Mangan

Director Ian Brown
Designer Tim Hatley
Lighting Designer Peter Mumford
Composer Richard Sisson
Sound Martin Slavin
Music Director Michael Tubbs
Company voice work Andrew Wade and Lyn Darnley

Characters

Peter
seventeen

Betty
twenty-one, his sister

Ann
twenty, his sister

Vi
nineteen, his sister

Mike
early fifties, married to Ann

Hugh
late forties

Rose
nineteen, Hugh's daughter

Time
Late spring, 1945

Setting
The living room of a flat in Clapham,
South London

For Zoe and Jocelyn

SCENE ONE

A large flat, Clapham, South London. Late spring, 1945.
*The living room; chairs, a sofa, two small tables, one
with photographs in frames. Three doors: one to the
outside hallway and stairs, one to a hall which leads to
two bedrooms and the WC, and one that leads to the
kitchen and the third bedroom (Mike and Ann's).*

*Ann, twenty and five months pregnant, sits on the
sofa, her feet tucked under her, reading a book, or
pretending to. Betty, twenty-one, fusses with the table.*
After a pause:

Betty I remember on Peter's eleventh birthday Father
turning on the gramophone, setting up chairs in a line,
telling us to keep walking, then – grab a chair when he
stopped the music. We couldn't stop playing the game.
It was hysterically funny, do you remember?

No response.

There was one less chair, so . . . (*Beat.*) Then it seemed
like the very next day Peter was gone.

Vi, nineteen, bursts in from one of the bedrooms.

Vi He's here! I just saw them out the window!

*Betty begins to fuss harder, mumbling, 'Oh God, oh my
God.' Vi rushes to the door, opens it, listens, closes it.*

They're coming up the stairs!

*Vi turns back to the room. She and Betty share a look.
Betty stops fussing and goes to her, takes Vi's hand
and holds it tightly in hers.*

Silence. Footsteps. The door opens. Mike (Ann's husband), fifty-three, enters with Peter, the girls' seventeen-year-old brother. He carries his suitcase. Ann has stood at a distance to watch.

Betty Peter! Oh my God, look at him! Look at you!

Betty and Vi rush him, hug him, they can't take their hands off him. Mike watches with a smile.

(*While hugging Peter with Vi, to Mike.*) Was the train late?

Mike (*shakes his head, then*) We missed each other. This photo you gave me . . . (*Holds up snapshot.*)

Betty (*pulling Peter*) Come in, come in. I've made you something to eat.

Peter I'm not –

Betty Mike has extraordinary connections. The things he finds. Look at these chocolate biscuits.

She has pulled him to the table. Peter notices Ann at a distance.

Vi She wouldn't let any of us touch them.

Betty Take off your coat.

Peter stares at Ann.

Peter (*smiles*) I didn't know – (*about the pregnancy*).

Ann One more surprise.

Peter (*to Mike*) Congratulations.

Mike I mentioned on the way here about work in the surgery. We could use another pair of –

Ann Later, Mike. Later. He's just got here.

Peter tries to stop Betty fussing.

Peter Betty . . .

He touches her hand, looks her in the eyes. She
suddenly turns away and begins to cry. For a moment
no one knows what to do. Ann goes and holds her.

Mike It's a small surgery. Just me and another doctor.
You'd get to do a number of things. Check in patients.
We need the help. It's not charity.

Ann Mike . . .

Peter Thank you.

Betty continues to sob on Ann's shoulder.

Mike Betty is our nurse.

Peter I know.

Vi Sit down, please, Peter.

Ann How was the journey?

Peter I missed a connection in Toronto. But I caught up.
I met two – 'boys' my age, who I hadn't seen since the
trip over. Strange.

Mike You were in –

Vi (*answering for him*) Alberta. (*Beat.*) That's the left-
hand side part. (*Looking at Peter.*) You look like Father.

She turns to Betty, who is trying to calm down and
who nods in agreement, staring at Peter.

Peter (*still standing with suitcase*) Should I put –?

Betty (*breathing deeply, wiping away her tears*) Mike
and Ann, of course, have Mother and Father's room. Vi's
moved in with me. So you have your old room back.

Peter I didn't need my old –

Vi Father's library and the bathroom we had to give up.

Peter (*confused*) When –? (*To Betty.*) You never wrote –

Vi (*explaining*) They're another flat now.

Betty What was there to write?

Vi Maybe in a while – Mike thinks – we might get them back. Put it all back together. We have the kitchen.

Betty (*still staring*) I used to bathe you. (*She smiles.*) Please sit down. (*To the others.*) He's a man.

After a beat, this makes the others laugh.

Vi What did you expect?!

The laughter dies down. Awkward pause – what to say after so many years?

Mike (*finally*) I'm looking forward to hearing about Canada. It's a place . . .

Peter That you'd like to visit?

Mike Not particularly. (*He smiles.*)

Peter (*to Ann and Vi*) And I'm interested in hearing all about Wales.

Ann What's to tell? (*She shrugs.*)

Peter And Vi, you're acting.

Betty (*to Ann*) Listen to his accent.

Ann I know.

Peter has an American/Canadian accent.

Betty (*answering Peter*) Did you ever think she'd do anything else?

Peter Mother would be pleased.

Betty I don't think so.

Peter Father?

They react, shake heads, laugh – of course he wouldn't be pleased.

Vi I had an audition this morning. Do you know *Autumn Fire?*

Ann (*over this*) It was on at the Duchess –

Betty (*over this*) We saw it – When did we see it?

Peter I don't know anything! I've been in Canada!

Laughter.

Betty It's very good.

Vi The part's Peggy. She's –

Betty (*over this*) Tell him who Peggy is.

Vi She –

Ann (*before she can explain*) Just do the bit. What you did for the audition.

Vi But he just got here.

Peter No, I don't – (*mind*)

Mike Which one is Peggy?

Betty Shhh.

Ann Show him.

Vi walks out, then returns as 'Peggy'.

Vi (*as Peggy*) 'Hen, dear. It's been ages.' (*Pretends to kiss 'Hen'.*) 'And Howard darling. You don't look ill at all. Or aren't you? (*Trying to figure it out.*) Or wasn't that you? Is that brandy we're drinking?' (*Takes a sip of 'Howard's glass'.*) 'Mmmmm. Thank you, I was nearly sober. And – who – is – that?' (*Points to an imaginary man.*) Hen says: 'Have you met my cousin, Peter?'

Betty (*making a connection where there isn't any, to Peter*) The character's name is Peter.

Vi (*as Peggy*) 'And where, Hen, have you been hiding such a man? Under your bed?' (*She holds out her hand for the imaginary man to shake.*) 'You – I'll see later.' (*As she walks across the room, to the imaginary Hen.*) 'A family secret, I suppose. Or is it – treasure.'

Mike I'm going to pour myself a drink. (*To Peter.*) Anyone –?

Betty He's only –

Vi as Peggy sinks into a chair.

Vi (*as Peggy*) 'There wasn't a living thing in all of Paris. Only the French.'

Betty (*to Mike*) He doesn't want a drink.

Peter notices the photographs on the small table, though he continues to watch Vi's audition.
Vi as Peggy sits, smoothing her crossed legs with her hand, as she continues:

Vi (*as Peggy*) 'What a simply horrid week abroad. Thank God for champagne, or I'd actually remember it.'

Mike laughs, then Betty does, looking at Mike. Ann watches Peter, who has picked up a framed photo, but is still watching.

'What possessed me? No, I shall never again stray. I make this my oath, upon pain of death, never again shall I venture forth off this great island of civility, of kindness and beauty, and into the filthy godforsaken seas which surround it.'

Ann (*to Peter*) Then one of the characters –

Betty (*explaining over this*) Howard.

Ann (*continuing*) – asks, 'So you'll never leave England again?'

Vi (*as Peggy*) 'England?! Who said anything about England? I was talking about – the Savoy.'

Laughter, and the audition is over. Peter sets the photo back down and applauds.

Ann (*teasing*) Maybe Mother wouldn't be happy.

Laughter.

Vi (*all shyness*) Peggy's supposed to be in her thirties. I told them I thought I was too young.

Betty You should let them decide –

Vi The tour's Grimsby, Warrington, Liskeard, and somewhere else, I forget. (*Beat.*) They'll let me know. Maybe this week.

She suddenly feels terribly awkward, everyone looking at her.

(*Embarrassed*) Why did I do that? Of all things to – He just got . . .

She turns away, quickly turns back to see Peter smiling and looking at her.

What? Why are you staring?

He suddenly goes and hugs her. This makes Betty start to cry again.

Peter Betty, please . . .

Betty Listen to that accent!

Peter I'm sorry, but . . .

Betty I didn't say that it was bad.

13

Vi breaks away, and being very much the child now:

Vi As long as Mother and Father don't find out.

She hurries to the photo Peter was looking at and turns it face down. Again laughter. Mike hands Peter a drink.

Mike Here.

Betty He's seventeen years old!

Mike (*sipping his drink*) My point exactly.

Peter What I'd love is a cup of tea.

Vi I'll put the kettle on –

Betty (*at the same time*) I'll get it – (*Turns to Vi.*) You do the kettle. I'll take his bag into his room. And see if the bed's made.

Vi I made it.

Betty And see if the bed's made – correctly.

Betty and Vi hurry off, leaving Peter with Ann and Mike. After another short, awkward pause:

Mike I'm standing there outside the buffet, holding up this photo – he goes by me – what, two or three times? (*He laughs and ruffles Peter's hair as if he were a boy.*)

Ann As long as it worked out – in the end. That's all that counts. (*She looks at Peter, then:*) Come here.

Vi (*off, she shouts*) I'm so happy!!

Ann (*to Peter*) Come here.

Peter goes to her and she holds him, strokes his hair.

I don't know what to say.

She turns back to Mike who now sits, smiling, sipping his drink.
   She turns back to Peter, begins to kiss his cheeks, rub his hair, hug him, repeating:

Look at you. Look at you. Look at you.

SCENE TWO

The same, later that evening.
   Peter sits, plate of food in his lap. The others have eaten, plates to their side or on the floor, or they have chosen not to eat.

Ann At first – they seemed really nice. I was treated like I was someone special.

Peter It was the same with me. Then –

Vi I didn't have this problem.

Ann That's not true.

Vi She talks about this and –

Ann You got as upset as I did.

Peter (*to Betty*) You started to feel like they were thinking, 'Is this kid ever going home?'

Ann (*to Vi*) I saw how they looked at you. And how they looked at me. (*To Peter.*) They adored the little ones.

Peter In Wales you had to work?

Vi Work! What else did we do? What else did I do? I practically took care of her.

Ann That's completely untrue! I was like – the mother, for God's sake.

Vi I don't believe this.

Ann From the moment at the station, standing there with our little luggage labels with our names on them around our necks. When Mother let go of my hand – she put it in yours. I knew what she was saying. I was fourteen years old! But I held on. When they tried to separate us – who screamed? (*Beat.*) Who took her fist and began hitting the lady who was trying to push my sister away into another queue? We're a family, I said. You can't separate us. (*Beat.*) We're all we have. (*Beat.*) This big house – the school was in one side, we slept in the other. This was for about a month. Then we billeted with a couple. We slept together. (*Beat.*) Vi and me. (*Beat.*) He was a miner. He'd have his bath – we'd get our 'uncle's' bath ready – by the fire, then – off we go. Get out. Into the winter, summer – outside. Off you go. And wait. Sometimes we went to the pictures. Until Mum and Dad . . . And we weren't being sent any more money.

Betty I sent you money.

Ann That's true.

Pause.

Vi They had a dog. A really nice dog – at the school. We loved the dog. A bit of a labrador. Black. He began to follow me around. (*To Ann.*) Remember? (*Back to Peter.*) I took care of him. He slept at the foot of our bed. (*Beat.*) I went to school. Came back. He was gone. He'd been volunteered to the army. Sniffing land mines in Belgium. I cried more than when Mum and Dad died.

Short pause.

Peter Just a couple of days after I got to my 'aunt and uncle's', their big black-and-white cat had kittens. Nine. I was so – happy. To see them. Some – things – that –

knew, understood – even less than me. (*Smiles, takes a bite.*)

Vi (*to Betty*) I know what he – (*means*)

Peter So my 'auntie', I suppose, seeing my – pleasure? She says, choose one, Petey.

Ann Petey?

His sisters giggle.

Peter It happened. I don't know how –

Betty Petey!!

Peter (*over their giggling*) Choose one! We'll have to drown the rest.

The girls stop giggling.

I look at those kittens in the barn. Each one. I touch each – one. And I couldn't choose. It wasn't right to choose, I felt. Auntie got impatient with me, and she drowned them all. (*Pause.*) When they put me in the field to work? I was put with some Negroes. I said to 'Uncle' – I'm a white man, I'm not a Negro. And he took the palm of his hand and rammed it into my head. I think I was passed out for about ten minutes. (*Beat.*) For weeks I thought about why he did that.

Betty He was probably trying to tell you that Negroes were just as good as white people. He thought you were –

Peter I thought of that. Sometimes I thought that was the reason.

Beat.

Vi Maybe he just didn't like someone questioning him.

Peter Maybe. (*Shrugs.*) In school there a kid hit me because he said I had an uppity accent.

17

Betty You don't have a –

Peter Then. I lost it. So maybe Uncle heard . . . (*Shrugs again.*) I never knew. (*Beat.*) I feel there's so much I don't know.

Ann (*agreeing with his confusion*) Were we supposed to work or not? Were we sent – to work? Was that part of the plan?

Vi We were sent to be safe –?

Ann Why did I have to work? Margaret Wells? She came with us. We were on the same train. We were at the same school. She didn't work. Her 'auntie' taught her things. She had, I think, two beautiful dresses that her 'auntie' embroidered . . . (*Beat.*) I've often wondered – did they put us together for reasons? How did they – match us? Did they know something about us – me? Or was it all –? When we got off the train . . . No one had bothered to tell me this. (*To Vi.*) You didn't tell me this –

Vi (*over this*) What?

Ann I'd obviously touched some soot on the train, and touched my face with my hand – I saw it later in a window – there was a streak of soot across my head. (*Shakes her head and smiles.*) Maybe when we were standing in the queue? Being – picked? If I hadn't had that soot on my face – would I have learned to embroider like Margaret Wells? Would I have been picked earlier, by someone else? (*Short pause. To Peter.*) You're not eating.

He holds up his plate, she takes it, looks at him, strokes his hair.

Peter I should go and unpack. (*He doesn't move.*)

Betty (*to Mike*) This must be boring for you.

Mike No, no. It's not. I'll get another drink. (*He gets up and goes to get a drink, stops.*) But just don't start blaming all those people. They interrupted their lives for all of you. They were heroes, in my mind. (*He goes off into the kitchen.*)

Betty (*to Peter*) He's a nice man. A good doctor.

Vi He pays for all (*this*) –

Betty I work.

Vi He and Betty.

Betty He's been very good to us all. Hasn't he, Ann?

No response. This catches Peter's interest.

(*To Peter.*) She's never satisfied.

Ann (*suddenly upset*) How dare you say that?!

Betty If I can't say it, then who –

Ann (*over this*) Shut up! I said shut up, Betty.

Peter (*over this to Vi*) What's . . .?

Vi ignores the question. Just as suddenly as this erupted, there is silence.

(*To Ann.*) How did you and Mike – meet?

Vi He works with Betty.

Betty (*correcting*) I work with him.

Vi Betty brought him home.

Betty To meet my sisters. I had a crush on him myself, then.

She laughs. No one else does.

Ann and he make a wonderful couple. You knew that right away. They'll have a wonderful baby.

Ann He's a nice man. As she says.

Betty Mother would have liked him. She would have approved. She was trying to become a nurse, you know.

Peter I didn't –

Betty First it was a schoolteacher, then after the three of you went away, it was a nurse. She hadn't got that far when . . . It's why she was out that day. (*Beat.*) Mike, it turns out – isn't the world strange? It turns out was there as well. So she could have been one of the people he helped pull out. He helped pull people out from under all the . . . (*Beat.*) I have often wondered . . .

Vi Father is buried in France. You knew that?

Peter nods.

Betty They sent us a ring. We don't think it was Father's ring.

Mike returns with a drink. For a moment no one says anything. As he passes, Mike strokes Ann's head; she doesn't respond.

Vi (*finally*) At school they had attached a bell to a tree. We were told that if we spotted any enemy parachutists to run and ring that bell. (*Beat.*) I could see the tree from my seat in the classroom. I used to daydream that like large snowflakes suddenly the sky was filled with parachutes. And no one else saw them. Everyone else was too busy – learning things. I ran out of the classroom. Reached the tree and the bell and began ringing it with all my strength. Soldiers suddenly arrived and captured all the bad people. Dad was always one of the soldiers.

Pause.

Peter *I* used to dream of you (*all*).

He stands and hugs each one in turn.

I should unpack.

He starts to go, but is stopped by:

Ann Vi was in a nativity play – playing Joseph.

Peter Joseph?!

Vi 'Uncle' drew with coal on my face to make the whiskers.

Ann She didn't know who Joseph was.

Vi (*same time*) I didn't know who Joseph –

Ann Then she's told he's – Mary's husband. And I tell her like Dad is Mum's husband. So she's there in the nativity, and everyone is watching, and she says: 'Mary, get me a drink.'

> *Peter and his sisters all say: 'Just like Father!' and laugh.*
> *Still smiling, Peter goes down the hallway to his bedroom. The others stop laughing.*
> *The sisters start to pick up the plates, etc.*

Betty He's got – so old.

Mike He's a boy.

Vi (*ignoring Mike*) I thought I'd faint when I saw him.

Ann He looks like Father.

Vi I see Mother.

Betty He used to be – He'd never sit still.

Ann (*over this*) He's tired. Think about what we look like to him.

Vi And the flat.

Ann It must be . . .

Vi (*to Mike*) God, it must be a relief for you – to finally have another man around! (*She smiles.*)

21

Mike He's a boy.

Vi (*over this*) Some – reinforcements against all us women!

Mike I haven't minded. In fact, I've rather enjoyed it.

He laughs, as do Betty and Vi. As Vi picks up a plate, he leans over and tries to 'pinch' her and she 'squeals' – all a game they've played before. Vi starts to head for the kitchen, laughing. As she goes, we hear Peter calling her: 'Vi!' She turns and hurries down the hallway to Peter. Ann shows no reaction to the pinching.

Betty (*to Mike*) So what do you think?

Mike He's a fine boy. I like him.

Betty I knew you would.

Mike And I think we should be able to find a place for him in the surgery.

Ann And not just sweeping floors, he needs to learn –

Mike I'll supervise his duties myself.

Betty Thank you.

Beat.

Ann I mean it, Mike. Don't make promises you can't keep.

This stops the room for a moment, then Betty turns to Mike.

Betty You've been so good to us.

Mike (*shrugs*) Remember I had a son. Not much older than your Pete.

Betty (*suddenly smiling*) Or Petey as we now must call him!

She laughs.

Suddenly Peter comes out of the hall wearing a full cowboy costume – chaps, hat, vest, spurs. He carries a couple of packages under his arm.

Peter (*bursting in*) Howdy, English folk!

Laughter.

And this is how they really dress in Alberta!

Ann I don't believe –

Peter Except on Sunday for church, then they wear their fancy clothes! Hat's out to – (*here*)

But he is interrupted by Vi who appears in Indian costume (her present from Peter). She has taken off her dress and put on a little Indian vest over her slip, hoisted up the slip and put on the skirt – looking sexy and a bit indecent. The others react, laughing.

Peter And here is Viohantas, Indian squaw! (*Turns to Betty.*) And this is for you, Betty. (*To Ann.*) And for you. (*Hands out their presents. To Mike.*) I'm sorry, but I didn't get –

Mike Please.

Peter And I didn't know about the baby when –

Betty (*opening her package*) Where did you get the money?

She opens the box, takes out a blouse. She immediately turns away, takes off her blouse and puts on the new one.

Mike (*during this*) I'm turning away.

The new blouse is low cut, exposing her bra.

23

Betty How's this?

Peter (*goes and touches her bra strap*) You can't wear that with it.

Betty (*stunned, to her sisters*) Since when did our brother become a woman's fashion expert –? (*But she turns, glances at Mike.*)

Mike I'm not looking!

She turns, takes off the blouse, then her bra, then starts to put the blouse back on. As she does, Ann opens her present – jewellery.

Ann It's gorgeous, Peter! Where did you –?

Peter It didn't cost much.

Vi (*getting into being an Indian*) Remember we used to ride on Betty? She used to give Pete and –

Ann Petey!

Vi (*grabbing Betty*) Come on! Around the room!

Betty (*adjusting her blouse, ignoring Vi*) What do you think? I don't think I could wear this out –

Vi Get down.

Betty gets down, but continues to 'ignore' Vi.

Peter (*to Betty*) Perhaps it's not meant to wear out, but rather – at home. With – whomever?

He smiles. She nods, smiles, catches a quick look at Mike, then turns away.

Betty I'll wear it around the house then.

Vi Come on, horsey. Let's go. Come on!

Vi is on the back of Betty who is down on all fours, though still seemingly oblivious to her.

Ann (*at the same time, holding the necklace*) Peter, help me put it on.

He goes to help. Vi now rides Betty, who constantly fiddles with the new blouse as her breasts are nearly uncovered (though no one seems to notice).

Vi (*on Betty*) Faster! Let's attack those Germans!

Peter I think she's mixing up her wars.

Vi Yahoo!

Ann (*to Peter*) I love it. (*Kisses him on the cheek.*)

Vi Petey! You're next! Come on! Give her a ride! Come on!

Betty (*to Mike*) He used to do this all the time –

Ann Come on!

She drags him to Betty. Vi gets off, Peter, reluctantly, gets on, though doesn't put his whole weight on her. Betty rides around, begins to buck (as she used to when he was a small child). Others laugh as he tries to hold on – then the phone rings. This calms everyone down. Mike takes the call, then:

Mike (*to Vi*) It's for you.

Vi takes it. Betty 'whinnies' quietly. Peter slaps her bottom as he would a horse.

Betty Oh really!

She suddenly bucks and he nearly falls off. Vi hangs up.

Vi I didn't get the part. The director.

Beat.

Betty I'm sorry . . .

Ann I thought you wouldn't hear until –

Vi He says he thinks I'm talented though. He wants to have lunch.

Ann He's after you?

Vi doesn't respond, then:

Vi And he's something like twenty years older than me.

Then she realises what she has just said in Mike's presence.

Mike God, then he must have a foot in death's door.

He smiles, others laugh. The faux pas is forgotten, or forgiven.

Ann (*suddenly, to Vi*) Do you remember that when we used to play hide and seek on rainy days, there was always a place that Peter would hide – and we never found him.

Betty I remember that.

Vi I don't remember.

Ann Maybe you were too young. Maybe she didn't play.

Vi I'm older than Peter.

Ann He was a boy.

Vi What's that –?

Ann Where was that place, Peter?

They look at him, then:

Peter Start counting.

Ann What –?

Betty (*over this*) What are we –?

Peter Count!

Ann looks at the others, then covers her face and begins to count. Peter and Betty start to go off and hide. Betty hesitates, then goes in a different direction. Peter goes off towards the kitchen.

Mike (*to Vi*) Hide!

Vi (*whispers*) Where?!

Mike (*whispers*) Anywhere?

He suggests behind the sofa. She hurries there, just as Ann finishes her count.

Ann Coming, ready or not –

Peter walks back in. The others look at him.

Peter It was behind the ironing board in the kitchen cupboard. There's a hole. It's still there. (*Beat.*) But I don't fit.

SCENE THREE

The same. The next morning.

Peter, barefoot, sits, his legs over the arm of a chair, a book in his lap. He had been reading, but has been interrupted by Vi, who stands in front of a mirror, straightening her clothes, fixing her hair. She wears her best clothes. As she fixes she talks:

Vi First this girl says to her 'family' that she can't take communion. Her 'auntie' is all upset – we have a heathen in the house! We've taken in a heathen! Then she has to tell them, well – it's because I'm a Catholic.

Betty enters, dressed. She carries toast on a plate.

So she can't take communion.

Betty (*who has heard the story*) But then she does.

Vi That's right.

Betty (*beginning to eat the toast*) And she writes to her mother and obviously –

Vi You weren't even there. (*Turns back to Peter.*) Writes to her mother and her mother writes to the local Catholic priest and he comes to the house. And the girl tells him that, yes, she's taken communion in the Protestant church and –

Betty And she rather liked it.

Vi And so the priest, he says to her, child you will never again be allowed to take communion in a Roman Catholic service. (*Beat.*) Ten years old and he excommunicated her.

> *She leans over and begins to draw a line down the back of her leg – to look like a stocking seam.*

Finally they had to find another family for her. She became – nervous.

> *She finishes the seam, and turns to Betty to explain her clothes.*

They're making a picture in Leicester Square.

> *Reaches for the newspaper, tosses it to Betty.*

Looking for people to be society. You have to bring your own clothes. Pays a guinea for the day. And lunch. (*Turns back to Peter.*) How did we get started talking about . . .?

> *Suddenly, with newspaper still in hand, Betty goes to Vi and tries to lift up her skirt.*

(*To Betty, pushing her hand away.*) What are you –? Stop it!

Peter Betty?!

Vi Get away from me!

Beat.

Betty (*explaining*) I just wanted to – to make sure she was wearing her drawers.

Vi Why wouldn't I –?!

Betty (*to Peter*) Her audition yesterday? She came home and told me – while you were waiting to go in, she was sitting next to a girl. Vi notices her lift up her skirt – to cross her legs – and nothing. (*She turns to Vi.*) So –? What?

Vi says nothing. Betty continues to explain.

So what does she say to Vi? You're staring at her and what does this 'actress' say?

Vi (*quietly*) 'We'll see who gets the part.'

Peter That's disgusting.

Betty Isn't it.

Vi That's not what it's usually like. And you don't have to tell everyone –

Betty He's your brother! And he's a man. What do you think about that – as a man?

Peter I said, I thought it was disgusting.

Betty He's disgusted, Vi.

Vi She didn't get the part!

Betty How do you know that? Did you get it?!

She reaches to look again under Vi's skirt.

Vi It's not even an audition. It's only an extra!

29

Betty flips up the skirt. Vi has her drawers on. Betty lets the skirt fall. Vi is upset, nearly in tears. She moves away from her sister.

I have to go. Excuse me. Where's my hat?

Peter gestures.

Betty Let me get the shopping money and I'll walk with you as far as the tube.

She goes to the kitchen. Peter and Vi look at each other for a moment.

Peter (*to say something*) Betty doesn't have to work today?

Vi The surgery doesn't open until noon on Tuesdays.

Peter But Mike left –

Vi He goes to the hospital on Tuesday mornings. (*Beat.*) Betty does the shopping on Tuesdays. Ann used to do it, but with . . .

Betty has returned with coat and bag.

Betty (*more explanation*) And I don't mind one bit either. Ann shouldn't be carrying heavy . . . anything. Mike wouldn't hear of it, for one. (*To Vi.*) He's so – thoughtful. Mike. Isn't he?

Vi nods.

We think Ann's the luckiest woman in the world. Don't we?

Vi hesitates, then nods. Short pause. Betty stands looking at Peter.

Peter What?

Beat.

Betty Seeing you there, like that – with a book. You know what I just remembered? What I just realised I miss? Sitting around – together – all reading together. To each other.

Vi When have we ever done that?

Betty (*staring at Peter*) Not for years.

Beat.

Vi Did Mother used to read to us?

Peter (*shakes his head*) No, Father did. (*To Betty.*) For what? About a month? He'd come home from the newspaper and he'd read to us. Religiously – for a month. Then it just stopped. (*He shrugs.*) Why?

Betty I don't know.

Vi How do you remember and I don't?

Peter (*over this*) It's a good thought. We should do it.

Betty Now that we're all together.

Peter Exactly.

Beat.

Betty I feel like I don't know anything.

Peter (*holding up his book*) I doubt if Zane Grey is going to make you feel –

Betty It's a start.

She turns, notices something about Vi's collar that isn't right, so she straightens it as a mother might. Then, without saying anything more, they leave.
Peter puts down his book, goes to the screen or clothes rack and tub that lean against a wall. Sets the tub upright, places the screen/rack around the tub, then heads off to the kitchen.

31

After a moment, Ann enters from her bedroom. She wears a dressing gown. She goes and sits on the sofa, stands, turns on the radio, quickly turns it off. Sees the leftover piece of toast, takes a bite.

Peter returns carrying two large buckets of water for his bath.

Ann God, are my sisters loud.

Peter Did we wake you?

Ann You didn't.

Peter I'm going to take a bath. Is that all –?

Ann You live here, Peter.

He smiles, nods, goes behind the screen and begins to pour the water in. Ann watches, then:

We had such a nice bath, remember? It had little feet and little claws. So you could pretend you were on some animal. Or flying bird.

Peter pours the second bucket.

Peter I never pretended that. (*Beat.*) But it was a nice big tub.

Short pause.

Ann But now we have a telephone. (*She looks at the phone.*) That's something good. Better. (*Explaining.*) Because of Mike and the surgery –

Peter I assumed.

Ann So we mustn't assume that everything just gets worse.

Peter looks at her. She looks away, rubs herself.

I think I pee twenty times a night. Did *I* wake *you*?

Peter (*as he heads back to the kitchen with the buckets*)
I slept like a baby.

Ann You're home.

   Peter's gone.

Peter (*off*) What?!

Ann (*calling*) I said you're –

   *She stops herself. Takes another bite of toast. Looks
   at Peter's book. He returns with another bucket.*

I said you're home.

   He looks at her. He's forgotten the conversation.

Never mind. Where's . . . ?

Peter Vi's gone to be in a picture. Betty's shopping. (*He
goes to pour the water into the tub.*)

Ann I used to go shopping.

Peter But now you have to be careful what you carry.

Ann Do I? Is that warm?

Peter I've been heating it on the stove. (*He goes again.*)

Ann (*continuing the shopping drift*) The queues are for
ever! You need the patience of Job!

   *Peter's gone. Ann continues but really to herself or no
   one.*

Or nothing else to do. And that is just the impression
you get standing in some of those endless queues – that
people now have nothing to do. (*Beat.*) Or nothing they
want to do.

   Peter returns with another bucket.

Peter So now Betty does the shopping. That must be great for you. (*He starts to go to the tub.*)

Ann (*holding up his book*) You reading this?

Peter Yes, I –

Ann (*reading the inscription*) 'To Petey from your Auntie Fay.'

Peter She gave it to me as a going-away –

Ann *Riders of the Purple Sage.* Kids' book?

Peter Not necessarily.

Ann Looks like a kids' book.

Peter It's –

Ann Do you miss her?

Beat.

Peter What?!

Ann Do you miss her? 'Auntie Fay'? (*More adamant.*) Do you miss being called Petey?! When you left we called you Peter!

Short pause. Peter goes behind the screen and pours the water into the tub. He comes out – sets down the bucket.

Full?

Peter Enough.

Ann What do you remember of Mother?

Peter is stopped by this.

Betty remembers – so much more than me. But then she was here. She wasn't sent away. She was the lucky one – right?

34

Peter (*after a beat*) Yes.

Ann Is that what you think?

Peter Ann –

Ann (*almost yelling*) That she was the lucky one?! I'll tell you about your sister. Put this in your head. (*Beat.*) When Mother took Vi and me to the station, Betty was with us, of course. She's told me, walking home with Mother, Mother all of a sudden fell on to the pavement and started sobbing. She hit her fists against a wall. She crawled. Betty, who wasn't very large – isn't, but certainly wasn't then – tried to pick her up. (*Beat.*) At sixteen she suddenly saw a lot. When Mother died, Father was home on leave. So when the telegram came, Betty had to read it – to Father, who because it was ever so slightly ambiguously written kept saying – 'But there's still hope, isn't there? Isn't there? Please tell me that there is hope.' (*Beat.*) So she had to convince him. Convince those two sky-blue watery eyes. Convince Father that Mother was – gone. (*Beat.*) Lucky her.

Peter I didn't –

Ann Take your bath.

    Peter just looks at her.

(*To herself, rubbing her eyes.*) I need sleep.

    She reaches over and turns the radio back on – dance music plays.

Young man, there are things you don't know . . . (*She shrugs.*) Come here.

    Peter comes to her.

Raise your arms.

Peter What? Why –?

Ann I said, raise your arms.

Peter is confused, but he raises his arms. She looks at him seriously, then suddenly tickles him hard in the armpits. He pulls away.

(*Laughing.*) You are such a sucker! You always were! Do you do everything anyone asks you to do?!

Peter looks at her totally confused.

Grow up. Take your bath. It's getting cold.

Peter turns and heads for the screen.

Not only does he sound like a Canadian. He's come back with the wits of one!

Peter stops, thinks of what to say, says nothing, then goes behind the screen to take bis clothes off and get into the bath.

Do you mind if I stay . . .?

No response. She listens to the radio for a moment. Behind the screen Peter is undressed. We hear him get into the water.

Did Betty tell you we're having company tonight?

Peter (*off, behind the screen*) Some doctor –

Ann I tried to tell Mike – your first full day here, why do we need –

Peter (*off*) He's trying to help me, Ann.

Beat.

Ann Hugh. That's the man's name. Hugh. (*Beat.*) Betty's been trying to hook him.

Peter (*off*) That's not the impression –

Ann (*over this*) And God knows I hope she does. Maybe then she'd move those doe-eyes of hers off my husband.

Peter (*off*) Ann, I don't want to –

Ann (*over this*) Not that he doesn't encourage her. Not that he doesn't encourage all of them. Wait till you see his other nurse – she looks like she's twelve. He likes them young, that should be clear. (*Beat.*) Isn't it?

No response.

Peter?

Peter (*off, behind the screen*) This doctor, Betty said, was invited so I could meet him. Mike's trying to give me a choice. This man needs help too.

Beat.

Ann Oh. So that's the reason he's invited. I'm sorry – I got it all terribly wrong.

Peter (*off*) Ann, Betty said –

Ann Oh, 'Betty said'. Betty said! Let me tell you something – you believe everything your sisters tell you, Petey, and I fear for your future.

Beat. Then Peter suddenly finds this funny and laughs. Ann smiles and laughs too.

Peter (*off*) I don't care why this Hugh is –

Ann Shhh! I like this.

A song has come on the radio she likes. It is 'Goodnight Children Everywhere'. Peter listens as well, so that for a moment we don't hear the water moving around.

Radio
Goodnight children, everywhere
Your mummy thinks of you tonight.
Lay your head upon your pillow,
Don't be a kid or a weeping willow.

Close your eyes and say a prayer
And surely you can find a kiss to spare.
Though you are far away
She's with you night and day.
Goodnight children, everywhere.

Ann (*over this*) Vi and I had a special signal when this
came on. We'd snap our fingers . . . (*she snaps them*) and
it meant 'Mother'. That I was thinking about Mother.
And . . . (*two snaps*) Father. No one else knew.

Radio (*song continues*)
Sleepy little eyes and sleepy little head
Sleepy time is drawing near.
In a little while
You'll be tucked up in your bed
Here's a song for baby dear:
Goodnight children, everywhere . . .

*The pain is nearly unbearable, finally Ann turns it off
before it finishes.*

Peter (*off*) They played that in Alberta too. Some
American lady sang it.

*Pause. Then from behind the screen Peter snaps his
fingers once. Ann nearly collapses when she hears. She
then snaps once as well.*

(*Off.*) When the letter arrived about – Mother, Auntie
read it to me. They'd sent it to her, to open it.

*We hear him play with the water, slap it – to do
something.*

Auntie read it out loud over the kitchen table, then
folded the letter very carefully, put it back into the
envelope, then handed it all to me. (*Beat.*) She kissed my
head and said, 'They are savages. In Europe, that's what
they are. No better.' And then she took me outside – into

their garden – and pointed to the mountains. 'There,' Auntie said, 'is a better world. Mountains don't lie. Mountains don't cheat. They don't murder. They don't make war.' And then we both cried.

Ann picks up the photo on the table and looks at her parents.

That night, she brought out photos of Mother.

Ann is amazed by the coincidence of picking up a photo and having Peter, who can't see her, mention photos.

Not at all like those on the table there. Of Mother and Auntie dancing. (*Beat.*) You knew that Mother had been a dancer –

Ann I think maybe I forgot.

Peter (*off*) Really? So maybe that's where Vi gets her acting –

Ann I don't know.

Beat.

Peter (*off*) In fur coats. With their arms around each other. Kicking out a leg. Auntie had spent two years in London. They looked like children. Mother and her. Younger even – than us. With big smiles on their faces. Auntie said they were best friends. For those two years. (*Beat.*) It's how Mother met Father – dancing.

Ann What??

Peter (*off*) According to Auntie. And she was there. (*Beat.*) There was another photo – they're in some costume with feathers, black shoes with a strap across –

Ann Maryjanes.

Peter (*off*) I kept asking Auntie – what's this? When was this? She said, she couldn't remember. She just had the photos. (*Beat.*) Then she pulled out one of us. Betty, Vi, you and me. I couldn't be more than two. (*Beat.*) There we were sitting in a drawer, thousands of miles away from here. (*Beat.*) I didn't even know Mother knew her. I thought she was a farmer's wife. Then she brought out the photos.

Short pause.

Ann I had to look through Mother's clothes. There was a dress – like that. With feathers. I thought it was . . . for a party. It's still in the cupboard . . .

She goes to talk to Peter behind the screen. We hear him splash as he tries to cover himself up.

Peter (*off*) Ann! (*Short pause.*) What are you staring at?

Ann Nothing. Nothing. (*She comes back out.*) I'll get that dress out. Wouldn't it be great if it is the one in the photograph you saw? (*She goes and looks in the mirror.*) I could try it on . . . (*Short pause.*) Mike thinks I'm going to stay fat.

Peter (*off*) You're not fat, you're pregnant! Did he say –?

Ann It's what he thinks. His first wife was terribly skinny.

Peter (*off*) I didn't know he had a first –

Ann She was young too. Then she got older. Why did you give Betty and Vi those pretty clothes and me a necklace?

Peter (*off*) What?

Ann goes again behind the screen.

Ann (*off*) Why did you do that, Peter?

Peter (*off*) Ann!!

Short pause.

Ann (*off, quietly*) What's that?

He has an erection.

Peter (*off*) I'm sorry.

Ann (*off*) Don't be. Me?

Peter (*off*) Ann, I'm trying to take a –

Ann (*still from behind the screen*) The first erection I ever saw, he was a miner, he was all black.

Peter (*off*) I don't want to know, Ann.

Pause.

Ann (*off*) You going to do something with that?

Peter (*off*) It'll – calm down.

Ann (*off*) Will it?

Peter (*off*) Not if you keep staring at it.

Ann (*off*) And if I touch it?

Peter (*off*) Ann, what are you . . .?

From behind the screen, we hear the water move around as Ann touches Peter.

Ann (*off*) If you don't want me to . . . say something.

Peter (*off*) Ann.

Ann (*off*) Something besides Ann.

She is masturbating him. The water sounds get quicker as her hand moves faster, then splashing, then he comes.
Silence.

Ann comes out from behind the screen, trying to dry the arm she has just had in the water. She is shaking.
She sits, unable to say anything. From behind the screen no sound whatsoever.

(*Finally.*) Mind if I turn on the radio?

She does. Music. We hear Peter get out of the bath. He puts on his trousers and comes out, holding his shirt. As he reaches Ann, she grabs his shirt.

Look at that. Let me darn it.

He stands uncomfortably, not knowing what to do with himself, with his hands, etc. Music continues on the radio.

(*With the shirt.*) My God, was there no one looking after you?

She gets the sewing box and sits. After a moment she looks up, smiles at him, then begins to darn.

(*As she sews.*) At school in Wales, there was this big sign – official poster from the government. 'What girls can do to win the war.' What jobs – like – (*Nods to her darning.*) 'Study your sewing machine,' it said. 'Snug slippers from old felt hats.' But we didn't have any old felt hats in Wales. Things to fix – so you wouldn't depend upon – I suppose your father. Get used to him not . . . there? 'When a drawer sticks –' Vi and I used to pretend that our 'drawers' were stuck –

Mimes underpants stuck. She looks at Peter, who smiles.

They can get a child to believe anything.

Peter comes up to her. He is still shirtless, sockless. He looks at her from behind, holds her shoulders. She sighs and leans back.

I'm sorry.

He touches her hair, then leans down and tries to kiss her.

No!!

She pushes him back and slaps his hand. He is very confused now.

No. (*She rubs her eyes, then:*) Some days I lie awake in bed and I think – but I'm still a child myself. What the hell am I doing having a baby? (*Beat.*) But I'll be a good mother. Won't I?

He hesitates, then nods.

I think I'm ready. I was like a mother to Vi for so long. (*Beat.*) And before that, before you – left – to you.

Peter I thought Betty mostly –

Ann We shared. She dressed you. (*Beat.*) I bathed you.

Suddenly the door bursts open and Vi enters. Ann and Peter nearly jump, and move quickly and guiltily away from each other.

Vi (*as she enters, noticing nothing*) It's raining! They won't be shooting outside. At least I didn't waste my money on the tube. (*She is off, down the hall to her room.*)

Ann (*to Peter*) Have you finished your bath?

Beat. Peter goes and turns the tub over into a drain. As the water pours out, Vi returns, having taken off her blouse. She carries another shirt. She wears a bra but doesn't seem in the least bit self-conscious in front of her brother.

Vi So what are you two doing today?

Ann I have some cleaning and washing –

Vi Peter, what about you?

Ann (*over this*) Mike's asked him to drop by the surgery this afternoon. See what he thinks.

Peter I don't think I'm ready for that yet. I think I want to take my time before –

Vi Then come to the pictures with me! (*She puts her arm in his, still both shirtless.*) I hate going alone. A girl alone – they come out of the woodwork. (*To Ann.*) Don't they?

Ann I wouldn't –

Vi (*to Peter*) Come on, protect me! I'll put my arm around you and pretend you're my big boyfriend. (*She laughs. She goes to get the paper.*) What's showing? It'll say in the . . . Where's –?

She sees the paper. Ann stands and heads off.

Peter Where are you –?

Ann I have a headache. I'm going to lie down. (*She starts to leave, stops.*) Vi?

Vi turns to her.

Peter's not a little boy any more. I don't think we should walk around like that in front of him.

She goes. Vi smiles, then looks at Peter and smiles, then as she looks through the paper, she rather self-consciously puts her blouse on and begins to button it.

SCENE FOUR

That night.
Vi sits at the upright, slightly out-of-tune piano, playing as the others sing. The others now include Hugh

44

(late forties) and his daughter Rose (nineteen). Betty is in the kitchen.

All *(singing)*
The Bells of St Mary's
I hear they are calling
The young loves
The true loves
Who come from the sea.

And so my beloved
When red leaves are falling
The love bells shall ring out
Ring out for you and me.

They finish, but Hugh, who has been standing and singing enthusiastically, starts one more chorus – alone. Vi plays for him. He has an okay voice, though obviously thinks it is a very fine one.

Hugh *(singing)*
The Bells of St Mary's
I hear they are calling –

He sits on the piano bench next to Vi and looks at her and smiles as he sings.

The young loves –

He puts a hand on Vi's shoulder.

The true loves
Who come from the sea.

Vi, without missing a beat, pushes his hand off her shoulder.

And so my beloved
When red leaves are falling –

He gestures for all to join in.

All (*singing*)
The love bells shall ring out –

Peter tries to catch Ann's eye, but she won't look at him.

Ring out for you and me!

As they finish, Hugh laughs and applauds the others. They laugh and applaud as well.
Mike, who has been holding a tray of drinks, begins passing them out. When Hugh gets his, he raises it to Peter:

Hugh And Pete, my boy – welcome home to England!

Peter (*under his breath, correcting*) Peter.

All Welcome home!

Those who don't have glasses reach for one, and the 'welcome home' sort of peters out around spilling drinks, clinking glasses, etc.

Ann And how we've missed him.

Peter suddenly turns to Ann, who turns away. Betty enters from the kitchen, carrying a cake.

Betty Did I hear 'welcome home'?

Reactions front the others: 'Look at this!' 'Oh my God!' 'It's beautiful!' 'A cake!' etc.

(*Over this.*) Four eggs went into this!

Vi (*explaining*) We pooled our coupons.

Betty It's just out of the oven.

Others smell.

Peter (*touched*) Thank you.

Betty It was Ann's idea.

Peter turns to Ann, hesitates.

Vi Go ahead and hug her. She's not going to bite.

Peter gives Ann a gentle hug of thank you.

(*To the others.*) Why are men like that with pregnant women? They think they're going to break them?

She laughs. Ann smiles, first at Peter, then at the others.

Mike (*about the cake*) Why are you showing him now? We haven't eaten.

Vi As if he couldn't smell it.

Mike What happened to surprises?

Betty We've had enough surprises.

Hugh (*over some of this*) A cake! So now we start to have cakes again! Now there's a sign that it's all over.

Mike I think it's just a cake.

Hugh I haven't even *seen* four eggs together since . . . Things are back the way they used to be!

Betty (*to Ann, over this*) Is that what a cake means?

Ann shrugs.

I'd better take it back.

Vi (*standing*) I can do that. Sit down, Betty.

Betty Supper will be ready – in ten minutes.

Vi takes the cake from Betty.

Peter (*to Betty*) Beautiful cake. Really.

Betty (*pinching his cheek*) For my baby.

Hugh (*to Vi as she starts for the kitchen*) I'm sorry about – putting my arm on . . . I didn't mean . . . It must have been a – reflex?

He smiles at her. This has got the attention of the room. Vi says nothing and leaves for the kitchen.

Mike What did you do?

Hugh At the piano, I touched her shoulder. She flinched – You'd think I'd . . . (*Laughs.*) I didn't mean –

Betty suddenly grabs his hand and puts it on her shoulder.

Betty Here. You can put it here. (*She laughs.*) All of us don't mind.

Others laugh. She wears her new blouse – without bra. Hugh catches a quick look down her blouse.

Hugh Nice blouse.

Betty (*turns to Peter and says a little too loud*) See!

Peter (*to Ann, confused*) See what?

Ann (*ignoring Peter*) All he gave me was a necklace.

She is wearing it. Rose turns and looks at it and smiles. Beat. Then, as Vi is out of the room:

Hugh She's a charming girl, Vi.

Mike She is.

Hugh Plays the piano – very nicely. (*Turns to Betty, whom he is still holding.*) She's the youngest?

Peter No, I am.

Hugh (*to Betty*) An actress too? I can see that.

Betty Why are we talking about Vi?

48

Ann (*to Rose*) What about you, Rose, any brothers or sisters?

Rose shakes her head. Hugh grabs her and hugs her – she barely lets him.

Hugh (*hugging Rose*) All alone in the world, poor baby. (*As he hugs her, turns to Peter.*) So you were gone – five years?

Peter Nearly six.

Hugh (*still hugging Rose*) My God, will our children ever forgive us?

Mike (*sipping his drink*) What choice was there? So what is there to forgive us for?

Betty (*looking at Peter*) Still – look at how well he's turned out. Except for the accent! (*Smiling, she goes to Peter.*) And we'll get rid of that! (*She starts tickling him.*)

Peter (*trying to get away*) Betty, stop it! Stop! Ann!

Ann doesn't move.

Rose I think he sounds like a movie star.

Betty A movie star! Oh that's even worse! (*She tickles him even more.*)

Hugh (*over this, nodding to Rose*) Her mother ran off with an American.

This quietens Betty.

(*To Rose.*) When was this? (*He smiles.*)

Rose You know very well.

Hugh (*continues*) August '43. A journalist. He comes to talk to me about the demands of surgery. At home. What we have to cope with. I told him – we work twelve-hour days. 'Don't you even come home for tea?' he asks. 'No, sir. Not these days.' Then for some reason – I come home for tea – and guess who's in bed with her mother? (*He laughs.*) So there he is, trying to put on his trousers and he's shouting at me: 'You lied to me! You lied to the press!'

Laughter. Perhaps Hugh laughs a little too hard.

Betty (*laughing, still a little giddy*) Father would have liked that. (*To Rose.*) He was a journalist.

Hugh (*to Rose*) She's where now? I always forget.

Rose No, you don't.

Hugh Cleveland, Ohio. I found a magazine with some pictures. Looks like a godforsaken place. (*Shrugs.*) But I'm sure she's right at home.

Short pause.

Rose (*quietly*) That's not how it happened.

Vi comes out of the kitchen, everyone turns to her.

Vi (*confused*) What?

Rose (*graciously*) You're an actress, I understand. You sing and play wonderfully well.

Vi smiles, but is still a little confused why she is the centre of attention.

Betty She was almost in *Autumn Fire.*

Rose Which one –?

Hugh (*interrupting*) Rose sings. (*Beat.*) Sing.

Rose Father –

Hugh Like a bird. And dances. (*Turns to Peter.*) When she was a kid, she used to pull up her skirt and really kick like she'd seen in the pictures. It was the sweetest thing – and sexy. (*To Rose, smiling.*) I can say that now.

Rose Father –

Peter I'm sure.

Hugh (*over this, continuing*) Now she's going to be a teacher. And that's very clever, isn't it?

Peter (*being polite*) How interesting –

Hugh (*over him, to Ann*) You know you've got lots of company, don't you?

Ann (*confused*) Company? What . . .?

Hugh (*to the room*) I don't think a day goes by – (*Turns to Mike.*) Does it?

Mike I don't know what you're –

Hugh (*continuing*) Without two, three, sometimes five, even six women coming in – pregnant.

Ann I do know two or –

Hugh (*not listening*) It's like a – what's the word I'm looking for?

Peter Plague?

Others laugh, then Peter laughs.

Hugh (*laughing*) No! Anyway, I figure – and I've talked about this with Rose – and I think she's listened – it's teachers that are really going to be needed now. Someone to take care of all these bloody babies. (*Beat.*) It's *the* field right now.

Betty Sounds like it.

Hugh And Rose has got it worked out so . . . Tell them.

Rose (*embarrassed*) Tell them what, Father?

Hugh That if – you – how it's not a waste . . .

Rose (*biting the bullet*) If I study to be a teacher and – and I get married, then, well, I haven't really wasted my time. I can put what I've learned into helping my own children.

Hugh (*rubs her head*) Clever, isn't she? And realistic. Did you know that there are nearly two girls for every boy right now? (*To Peter.*) Maybe you shouldn't be hearing this. (*He laughs.*) For every healthy boy. So you've got to be realistic. (*Beat.*) Betty's realistic.

Betty Am I?

Hugh I've seen you at Mike's side. He'd better be careful or I'll steal you away! (*Laughs.*)

Betty (*over the laughter*) Please, steal me away!

More laughter. She catches Mike's eye.

Mike (*joining in the 'joking'*) You'll have to fight me first!

Betty (*smiling*) Is that really true?

The laughter subsides, then:

Mike Seriously, Betty's a fine nurse. Any surgeon would be lucky to have her at his side. (*He looks at Betty, then 'presents her'.*) And she cooks!

Peter laughs, thinking this is still the joking, but no one else does. Suddenly the conversation has taken a more serious tone.

Hugh I'm looking forward to supper. (*Turns to Betty.*) And that is a very handsome blouse.

Betty Thank you.

Mike She manages the whole household. Doesn't she?

He turns to Ann and Vi, who say nothing.

Betty And I keep the books.

Peter (*confused*) What is –?

Ann Shhh.

She hits him to be quiet. Hugh stares at Betty, who stands perfectly still.

Hugh (*finally*) And you're the oldest.

Betty nods.

Usually the oldest is the most responsible. Most trustworthy.

Mike When Ann and Vi returned from Wales – Betty was like their mother. She did everything. (*He looks Betty over again.*)

Hugh I can't believe you wouldn't miss her, Mike.

Mike I know I would.

Short pause.

Betty (*finally*) Dinner should be ready. Excuse me. (*She goes off to the kitchen.*)

Peter (*half-whisper to Ann*) Isn't he going to look at her teeth?

Ann Shhh!

Mike (*to Hugh, as he fills his glass*) Always the responsible one. She runs the surgery for me, Hugh. There are days when I think why did I even bother to come in.

Beat.

Rose Are you looking for a nurse, Father?

No response. Suddenly Hugh turns his attention to Vi.

Hugh But you – you are a wonderful singer. And I love – to sing. As you probably figured out.

Vi (*barely hiding the lie*) And you sing very well.

Hugh Thank you.

Rose If a little too loudly.

They laugh. Hugh turns back to Vi.

Hugh You sing. You play. You act?

Vi Yes.

She stands, feeling awkward, caught in his stare.

Ann When we were at school, Vi won third prize for her singing.

Hugh Only third prize?

Vi This was in Wales.

Hugh Of course. What sort of plays do you like to act in?

Vi doesn't know how to answer.

I've always thought that backstage in a theatre must be one of the most – I don't know . . . There must be a real kind of excitement. Of life. Actors rushing around, changing costumes – right off the stage, I'm told – Waiting. Anticipating. Then! (*Slaps his hands.*) I've had two patients who were actresses. I know something about acting.

He stares at her, then she goes and sits. He turns to Ann.

And you, Ann, we haven't said a word about you.

Ann I don't think Mike will let you steal me away.

Laughter.

Will you?

More laughter.

Hugh (*looking at her*) I haven't delivered enough babies. I should deliver more. (*Beat.*) They're inducing more and more now, aren't they, Mike? It's so much easier to schedule that way. You go from one to the next, I'm told. And it's even safer for the mother, isn't it?

Mike As soon as her waters break, we plan to induce.

Vi (*to Ann*) Do you know about this –?

Ann Mike's told me what to expect.

Mike Which isn't much. We'll put her under. She won't feel a thing. She won't even know what's happening to her.

He takes Ann's hand and squeezes it. Hugh suddenly turns to Peter.

Hugh Rose here, Peter, is also a very good cook.

Rose Daddy!

Peter That's – (*nice*)

Hugh And smart as a whip.

He points to her head. Betty suddenly bursts out of the kitchen, wearing Peter's cowboy hat, and announces:

Betty Dinner is served!

The others react to the hat: 'What's that?' 'Peter's', 'Take it off'.

Hugh (*as they are going, to Betty*) That's what I imagine my wife wearing now.

Rose I don't think they wear cowboy hats in Cleveland, Ohio.

Vi Is that where she – ?

Hugh suddenly interrupts by putting his arm around Vi and whispering something.

Go ahead, if you want.

Mike stops Peter.

Mike Peter, can you help me collect the glasses?

As the others head off, Hugh breaks into another chorus of 'The Bells of St Mary's'. Only Betty joins in. They are off. Peter starts to collect the glasses.

Do you like Rose?

This stops Peter.

You don't mind that she's here.

Peter Why would I mind?

Mike Good. She's just a little older than you, I think. But probably not nearly as – experienced?

He tries to smile, Peter looks at him, is about to say something.

(*Biting his nail.*) Ann talked to me about this morning.

Beat.

Peter What about this morning?

Mike (*seemingly changing the subject*) Today in surgery there was Mrs Jones. She was with her husband – Mr Jones. (*Smiles at the obviousness of this and continues.*) She's been fainting. Dizzy. You could see the disease in her eyes, Peter. They both looked at me, expecting. Hopeful. This man had served his country. (*Beat.*) I knew

56

she was dying. I could have told them this. (*Beat.*) They could have spent the next – months? Building memories? I could have begun this for them. But instead, I said . . . something like, 'Your wife, Mr Jones, has a thirty to forty per cent chance of extending normalcy through this year.' 'Thirty to forty per cent?' I heard him say. 'Better than we had hoped.' Translated, what I said meant – she might maybe live through the remainder of this year – these next seven months, but probably not. But they heard something different. I'm a coward, Peter. I can't . . . It's not in my nature, I think . . . Don't hate me for that. (*He smiles – at his own exaggeration. Then, holding out his arm:*) That's me! Now you know me!

He smiles. The singing from the kitchen has stopped. Ann appears.

Ann Mike? Peter?

Mike In a minute.

Peter looks at Ann, who returns to the kitchen, from where we start to hear 'The White Cliffs of Dover'. Mike sighs, this is obviously very difficult for him. He sighs again, then:

She told me about seeing you in the bath and what that made her feel, Peter. (*He tries to smile.*) And then you sent her back to her room. Thank you. A child's punishment for a child's . . . (*Beat.*) Good for you. And that is what happened.

Peter Are you telling me –?

Mike And that is what happened. (*He stares at Peter. Then:*) Women when they are pregnant, Peter – I speak as a doctor – well, they don't always do the rational thing. That's an understatement. (*Smiles.*) So it's up to us. To help them out. Not let their – emotions – get the best of them. (*Beat.*) She was embarrassed when she told me. Even contrite. Now I suspect she's forgotten the whole thing. As should you. As will you. (*Suddenly a big smile.*) Come here! Here.

Grabs him and holds his head.

God, I know this can't be easy. But know that you have me. All right? Any time you want to talk. Need an ear.

Steps back, holds open his arms as he did before.

That's me!

Vi (*off*) Mike!

Mike Coming! (*Slaps Peter's shoulder.*) I'll get Rose to help you with those . . . (*The glasses.*)

Peter I don't need any –

Mike She's a good-looking girl.

He winks and goes. Peter picks up a few glasses. Rose appears.

Rose I'm supposed to help . . .

From the kitchen we hear: 'Are we eating?' 'Start serving', etc.

Are those all the glasses?

He hands her one.

Thanks. I suppose we should take them back in the kitchen. (*Beat.*) Do you ever go to the pictures? I love the pictures. I never say no to anyone who asks me to go to the pictures.

Peter hesitates, then, without saying a word, heads for the kitchen. Rose, a little hurt, follows.
Off we hear their arrival: 'At last!' 'Now can we eat?' etc.

And the scooting of chairs being moved around the table, the murmur of talk. Then the clinking of a glass as Mike tries to get everyone's attention for grace.

Mike (*off*) Dear God, Father of us all, we ask You to bless this our table and we, Your children . . .

SCENE FIVE

Later that night.
Radio is on – the glow of the yellow dial is the only light visible. Ann sits alone, curled up in a chair, smoking.
Noise off, footsteps, voices, etc.
The door to the outside hallway opens. Vi, Betty, Peter and Mike enter, talking.

Vi (*teasing*) Come on. Come on, Betty! Say what you think of him! (*To the others.*) She won't say. Why won't she say?

Peter (*to Ann*) You're sitting in the dark.

They start turning on lights.

Vi Is he your type? Is he not your type?

Betty He's not my type.

Vi He's not her type.

They are taking off their coats, etc.

Well, I thought he was sort of good looking.

Betty I know you did.

Vi What is that supposed to mean?

No response.

Ann (*to Mike*) What happened?

Vi (*continuing*) So – I think you're making a mistake.

Betty What sort of mistake am *I* making, Vi?

Mike (*to Ann*) About Hugh.

Vi A doctor. Not bad looking. Divorced.

Still teasing, Vi winks at Peter.

Betty You don't know anything.

Vi (*smiling*) I think she fancies this man, that is exactly what I think.

Betty (*upset, but the others don't see this yet*) He's looking for a nurse! (*Turns to Mike.*) Did you know that? I couldn't just leave you.

Mike (*smiling*) You do what you want.

Turns to the others and smiles. Leans over and kisses Ann on the head.

How's the headache?

Ann I'm all right.

Betty (*erupts*) So I just do what I want?! I don't think I even know what that is any more! I think I've forgotten even what that means!

Ann (*concerned*) Betty –

Betty (*very upset now*) I think it's been beaten out of my skull! I think all I know now how to do is take care of people! Do what you want!!

Vi suddenly smiles. Confused, she turns to Ann.

(*To Vi.*) Go ahead and laugh at me!

Vi I wasn't laughing at –

Betty (*then it comes out*) He was all over you, Vi.

Vi What?!

Betty And you encouraged him!!

Vi I did no such thing.

Betty You selfish little girl. You've always been so selfish!

Ann Stop it, Betty! Stop it!

Betty (*over this*) I saw you crossing your legs. We're talking about something else and suddenly – it's legs. How he likes legs! (*Beat.*) I hate my legs. I hate them.

> *She starts to cry and runs off to her bedroom. The others are stunned, having had no idea how serious this was.*

Ann What . . .?

Vi I did nothing. Nothing!

Ann Something must –

Vi I think the guy's a joke. A moron. Why would I try and pick him up? (*Beat.*) She's insane. (*Shrugs.*) She shouldn't drink.

Peter She hardly drank anything.

Vi (*yelling*) Then I don't know what her problem is. Don't blame me!

Mike (*quietly*) She must have heard . . .

Vi What?

> *Beat.*

Mike Hugh and I were talking – I told him to – shhh. And Betty was walking back from the Ladies. He looked at her – he said he thought her ankles were thick. (*Beat.*) I didn't think she heard . . .

Ann He said that?

Mike (*making light of it*) We were looking at all the girls. Not just Betty. This one's nose is too small. This one's . . . you know. (*Suddenly remembering.*) He liked her breasts. He said – Betty's got nice breasts. But thick ankles. So it was sort of – balancing: this is good, this is not as good . . . (*Beat.*) He didn't mean anything by it. In his defence, he . . . (*Shrugs. Pause.*)

Ann She must like him.

Vi Not necessarily.

Ann True.

Suddenly the phone rings. They look at each other, then Vi picks it up.

Vi (*into phone*) Hello? Oh . . . I'll look. (*She covers the receiver.*) It's the tactful – Hugh. He's lost his hat, he wonders if he left it here.

They immediately see it on a table. All point. Vi starts to uncover the receiver, then has a better idea. She sets the phone down and goes to the hallway and calls.

Betty! Telephone! Betty! Betty!!

Betty appears, very hesitant.

It's – Hugh.

Betty starts to go back. Vi grabs her.

He's lost his hat. It's right over there. Tell him.

Betty tries to leave again, Vi holds her.

Tell him!

Suddenly her sister and brother see what Vi is doing and join in: 'Tell him, Betty! Please, Betty! Tell him!

62

Tell him!' Even Mike joins in, but without really knowing what is going on. Ann, Vi and Peter plead: 'Betty!'

Betty finally goes to the phone, picks it up.

Betty Hello? . . . It's Betty. Your hat's here.

She starts to hang up. But Hugh has said something.

What? . . . Thank you. It was Mother's recipe actually . . . I'll write it down if you like and post it . . . What? (*Beat.*) Tomorrow? . . . Let me think. (*To the others.*) Am I free tomorrow night?

The others just stare at her.

Yes, I think I am free. That would be very nice indeed. Thank you so much. Goodnight. (*She hangs up. Short pause.*) He asked me out. On a date. I think I'll do the washing-up now. (*She turns and starts to go, then stops and speaks to Mike.*) He's a nice man. I like him.

She smiles, turns to the others and tries to make a joke.

(*Patting Mike*) And if I can't have Father here, then I'll have to settle for Hugh.

Then she realises what she has just said.

Peter (*quietly*) Father?

Betty (*embarrassed*) I mean – Mike. Mike here. I'm just joking, Ann. (*She tries to laugh. Then, to say something:*) He's taking me to dinner. Hugh.

She goes. No one says anything for a moment, then:

Vi I'll help Betty.

Mike What was all that about? Sometimes I walk into this house and I feel I don't have a clue about what's going on.

63

He turns to Ann, and Peter near her.

Peter I should probably get to bed.

Vi (*goes to Peter*) Funny, your sisters, aren't they? (*She kisses him on the cheek.*) Thanks for taking me to the pictures.

Peter (*to Ann and Mike*) I'm sorry to report I didn't have to fight anyone off! (*He smiles.*)

Vi And thanks – for coming home. Goodnight. (*To Ann and Mike.*) I'll help Betty do the washing-up. Night.

Ann Goodnight.

Vi goes into the kitchen.

Vi (*off, to Betty*) So I'm a selfish little girl, am I?

Betty (*off*) I'm sorry, I didn't mean –

Vi I'm joking, I know –

Door closes and we don't hear any more.

Ann (*to Mike*) I won't be long.

Mike I'll get myself another –

Ann You've had enough to drink. Go to bed. Peter can keep me company.

Peter is surprised by this. Mike looks at him. Nods, then:

Mike I'll read.

He goes.

Ann I think he has a girlfriend. His nurse. (*Beat.*) What do you think?

Peter shrugs and goes to the bottle on the tray.

What are you doing?

64

Peter I want a drink.

Ann You're seventeen years old! And I don't know what Mike is doing taking you to a pub –

She tries to take the bottle away, Peter holds it out of her reach.

Peter Father gave me my first drink years ago. Right in this room.

Ann What are you talking about –?

Peter I was ten, I think.

Ann suddenly realises.

Ann Oh my God, are you drunk?!

Peter (*over this*) He poured me a beer. Then another. Then a third and I threw up. He said, 'Son – if you're going to drink, then I want you to learn how to drink, right here in your home.' (*Beat.*) Well, I'm home.

He pours himself a drink. Beat. Points towards the kitchen.

Maybe I should help.

No response. He sits.

I want to go to bed. (*He sips his drink.*) Why did you talk about this morning with Mike?

Ann Because . . . (*shrugs*) he's my husband? I don't know. (*Beat.*) But I didn't tell him what happened. Because nothing happened, Peter. We have to face that. Accept that. (*Beat.*) Mike was terribly interested – in my feelings. He was almost sweet about it. (*Beat.*) I think it was the doctor in him.

Peter (*interrupting*) I could have stopped you, this morning, you know.

Ann Stop what? What happened? You sent me to my room. A naughty, naughty girl. (*Suddenly.*) It was a dream! I'm not a freak! I hate it that you're drinking by the way. I really hate it.

He sets down his glass.

So – how was little . . . what's-her-name?

Peter Who?

Ann Hugh's –

Peter Rose.

Ann I knew it was some – form of vegetation. (*Beat.*) She was a late addition to the night, did you know? Mike asked Hugh to bring her along for you. (*Beat.*) After our talk – his conclusion was that you needed a date. Did you know that she was your date?

Peter Yes.

Ann Oh. (*Beat.*) I look at you and see a ten-year-old boy. I've got to get used to this. I thought she was dear. Sort of. Maybe you should ask her out. Or maybe you have? I've got a little pocket money, you could take her to the pictures. She obviously likes the pictures. Let me give it to you . . .

She gets out of the chair and goes to get her purse. Peter stops her, holds her arm. She shakes him off.

No.

Peter suddenly erupts.

Peter What game are you playing with me?!

Beat.

Ann No game. None. (*She stares at him.*) I'm trying to be – good. I'm trying to close my eyes and say: 'Mother,

66

please tell me what to do?' (*Beat.*) There is no one in the world I'd rather hold – than you. To hug. To touch. I want you pressed against me. Breathing each breath with me. (*Beat.*) I see the boy. I see – the brother. I see the man. Like pages in a book flicking by – faster and faster. Never stopping. All blurring into the next, Peter. All – at the same time. (*Beat.*) I love you so much.

Short pause.

Peter And what does Mother say?

Laughter from the kitchen. Ann looks at him, then shrugs. Peter leans over and kisses her on the cheek.

Ann Tell me – was that a brotherly kiss? Or . . . Tell me, Peter, because otherwise I should hit you. Should I hit you? (*Suddenly turns away.*) Remember having to line up in the kitchen, when we'd all done something wrong? Mother had that big wooden spoon. Where was Father?

Peter Probably drunk.

Ann Probably on business. (*Continuing.*) You were the youngest. So you were the last. And by then Mother would always say, 'Now I think I've made my point.' She couldn't strike you. Her daughters – no problem.

Peter I remember being hit –

Ann By us! We hit you, Peter! We took you out into the garden and gave you a good beating!

She laughs. Betty and Vi come out of the kitchen, laughing, the best of pals now.

Betty We're leaving the rest till morning. And I don't care if that's a sin! (*Noticing Ann and Peter smiling.*) What?

Vi They were always the closest.

Betty That is true, isn't it.

Vi I used to be jealous.

Peter (*explaining*) Ann was telling me how you'd take me out to the garden –

Ann (*same time*) When Mother wouldn't hit him! With his cricket bat!

Peter Cricket bat?

Vi Betty held you down.

Betty I was the strongest!

Vi And I made a little mark with my fingernail on the bat. For every smack –

Betty You hated that, so we kept doing it.

Peter I don't remember the bat.

Vi I'm sure it's here somewhere. This family throws nothing away. (*To Betty.*) Do we?

Betty (*to Ann*) By the way, I'm sorry about earlier . . .

Ann Please.

Vi (*going up to Peter as if to kiss him on the cheek*) Goodnight. (*She suddenly tickles him.*)

Betty He was always a sucker. Goodnight, little brother!

Peter Goodnight.

They are halfway down the hall.

Ann (*calling*) I'm going to bed too!

Vi and Betty are gone. Peter and Ann are again alone. Pause.

(*As if picking up the old conversation.*) Anyway, I'm ugly. A handsome boy like you – why would you want me?

Peter looks at her.

Peter You're the most beautiful woman I know.

Short pause.

Ann Have you ever had a girlfriend?

Peter hesitates, then shaking his head:

Peter No.

Short pause.

Ann Not even – 'Auntie Fay'?

Peter (*seriously*) Stop it.

Ann Sorry. It was a joke. Come here. Come here.

Peter approaches her. Stops.

Peter Are you going to tickle me?

Ann smiles, and shakes her head. She takes his head and presses it against hers. She kisses his cheek, his ear, his neck, then looks at him.

Ann At least I have better legs than Betty.

This suddenly makes them both laugh, and equally suddenly this laugh turns into a passionate kiss. They pull away, breathless.

I'll come to your room with you.

Peter But –

Ann Mike's asleep. I'm sure he's asleep. (*Beat.*) I'll just check.

She hurries towards her bedroom, leaving Peter alone. He waits, touches his face, sighs, bites his nails. Then, after a long pause, Ann returns.

(*Without looking at Peter.*) Mike wants another drink.

She pours a drink and exits.

SCENE SIX

The next morning.
    Peter, barefoot, but dressed, sits on the sofa, pretending to read his book.

Betty (*off, from her bedroom*) Vi! I hate this! I look like I don't know what! Vi!

    Vi comes out of the kitchen.

Vi I'm coming . . .

    Mike is right behind her. He holds his teacup.

Mike Will you tell her we have to go –?

Betty (*off*) Vi, help me!

Vi (to *Mike*) Tell her yourself –

Mike (*over this*) Betty! We have to –!

    Betty enters from the bedroom. She wears one of Vi's tight-fitting dresses.

Betty (*entering*) I can't even bend over in . . . (*She tries, stops.*)

Mike I like it!

Betty I'm not going to believe a word you say.

    She smiles. Mike laughs.

Mike (*'innocently'*) Why not? (*He laughs and winks at Peter.*)

Betty (*turns to Vi, about the dress*) Look, you can actually see the crease in my bottom.

    Mike 'leans over and looks' and winks at Peter.

Vi Is that bad?

Betty (*over this*) I can't walk in it. What else have you got? (*She heads for the bedrooms.*)

Mike Betty, we have to go to work! Can't you do that –?

Betty When? I get off at six. (*Turns back to Vi.*) In this he'll think I'm a bloody whore.

Vi (*as she and Betty go*) I very much doubt that.

Vi and Betty are gone.

Mike (to *Peter*) Extraordinary. In the surgery – she's like a rock.

He looks at his watch. Ann has entered in her dressing gown.

There she is! Sleeping Beauty awakens! (*To Peter.*) There's something to be said for a house full of women, isn't there? (*Back to Ann.*) She walks. She talks. Or does she?

Ann Good morning.

She kisses Mike on the cheek as she passes him. She goes to the sofa.

(*To Peter.*) Is there room there?

Peter moves and she sits down.

(*To Peter.*) Morning.

Mike Cup of tea?

Peter (*starting to stand*) I'll get you one.

Ann (*stopping him*) No, no, please. I don't want anything.

Peter sits back down. Ann pats his knee.

How did you sleep?

*Betty and Vi burst back into the room. Betty is now in
her underwear. She holds a blue dress in front of her.
Vi holds another dress.*

Betty Ann, which do you think, the blue or the green?

Mike Betty, I'm leaving in two minutes.

Peter Wasn't the blue one Mother's?

This stops everyone for a moment.

Betty Was it?

Peter I'm pretty sure.

Vi I think it was, he's right.

Beat.

Betty Then it's the blue one. Mother would have liked
that.

Vi The hem's too low though.

*She leans down and pulls up the hem, revealing more
and more of Betty's leg.*

How's this? (*Higher, teasing.*) How's this?

Betty Stop it!

Vi He'd like it like that. We know he likes legs.

Others laugh, Betty pretends she didn't hear it.

Betty (*to Peter*) You really remember Mother in this?

Peter I think so.

*Betty sighs, presses the dress against her chest and
starts to head back to her bedroom. As she turns,
Vi notices a hole in Betty's underpants.*

Vi Betty, you can't wear . . . (*She sticks her finger in the
hole.*)

Betty (*hitting her hand away*) What are you doing?

Vi (*sticking her finger back in the hole*) There's a hole. You can't wear these –

Betty He's not going to see my –

Mike (*over this, turning*) I'm not watching!

Vi (*over this, to Betty*) Are you so sure of that?!

Betty hurries out of the room.

(*To the room.*) Really, it's like dressing a child.

She follows Betty off.

Mike (*calls*) I'm going, Betty! Tell her I've gone.

He goes to the sofa, leans down and kisses Ann on the head. She rubs his arm with her hand.

(*To Ann.*) I forgot to tell you, Hugh mentioned last night that there might be a flat available in his building. I'll try and find out more.

Ann freezes.

Peter What?

Mike Ann and I have been looking for our own –

Ann No we haven't. Not for months.

Mike We just didn't find any –

Ann We decided to stop looking. We liked it here –

Mike (*over this*) We need our own flat!

Suddenly Ann and Mike are shouting at each other.

Ann My sisters are here and my brother!

Mike Your sisters could have their own rooms!

Ann And when the baby's born –

73

Mike That's my point!

Ann – to have aunts and an uncle – to help, Mike!

Mike I'm going to look at the flat!

Ann (*waving her arms, gesturing to this flat*) And who'll pay for –?!

Mike I will pay, dammit!

Pause. Mike looks at Peter, who turns away.

Ann This is an important conversation, we just can't –

Mike I have to go.

Ann You're always doing this –

Mike Goodbye.

He goes. Short pause. Betty hurries out of the bedroom, now in her nurse's uniform.

Betty Where's –? (*She looks around, realises Mike is gone.*) Bye. Goodbye. See you tonight.

She quickly kisses Peter on the top of the head, touches Ann's shoulder and hurries out after Mike. We hear her footsteps down the steps. Vi appears in the doorway.

Vi She's like dressing a doll. She has that much knowledge of clothes.

Ann Well, I'm sure you helped . . .

Vi I tried. I did my best. (*She starts to put on a jumper.*)

Ann Where are you going?

Vi Into town. They might be filming that picture in Leicester Square. It's not raining today. (*Beat.*) You two going to be okay?

74

Peter Yes. I think so.

Vi Don't wait on her, Peter. She's stronger than she looks. And she's more than capable of taking advantage. I can swear to that.

Ann (*smiling*) Be quiet.

Peter (*smiling*) I'll – be careful.

Vi goes to the door, stops.

Vi You don't feel I'm abandoning you, do you?

Peter You have to work. And Ann's here. And we did go to the pictures yesterday.

Vi True. That's true.

Ann Now it's my turn – to be with him.

Vi Right. Good. See you later then.

And she is gone, leaving Peter and Ann alone on the sofa.

Ann (*quietly*) Bye. (*She turns to Peter, then turns away and stands.*) So . . . I hate Mike.

Peter looks at her.

You heard him. Sometimes I hate him. And sometimes I say to myself, you shouldn't stay with someone you hate. And I believe that. (*Shrugs. She picks up Mike's teacup.*) Tea?

Peter shakes his head. Ann starts to head off for the kitchen, then returns right away.

Father used to do that to me. (*Beat.*) I remember once, he had a taxi waiting. I helped him down with his bag. He let me. He helped me help him. And as he was getting in – after a glance at the ticking meter – he said,

'Ann, I've decided which school you're going to.' Then taxi door slam and he was gone. No discussion. Nothing. (*Beat.*) Like you're a – thing to be told. Like you are nothing. (*Beat.*) I'm going to clean today. You can help me. Move the chairs around, that sort of thing. (*Short pause.*) It's because of you that Mike's looking for another flat. Suddenly we're – 'crowded'. (*Beat.*) All I ask is for the opportunity to talk about things. Before decisions are made. Before things are done, and can't be – reversed. (*She looks at Peter.*) You are so young. I can't believe how young you are. (*Beat.*) So what are we going to do today? Should we talk about it? (*Short pause.*) I love this flat. I must know every inch. (*Pointing to the sofa.*) I remember – God knows how old I was – certainly not old enough to 'get it' – but I came around that corner. And there were Mother and Father on that sofa. Right there, Peter. Her blouse was – it was hanging off her shoulder. She was sitting on Dad. (*Beat.*) The upholstery is the same as it was then. We haven't changed it. (*Beat.*) I'm not going to the pictures with you. I've stopped all that. You can go yourself if you want. (*Short pause. She thinks, then:*) You step outside today – just one foot out of your home – and it all makes no sense any more. And it's been building up to this for a while. (*Suddenly remembers.*) About a month ago, I was out . . . You know the shop – it used to be a greengrocer's near the surgery on the High Street? Of course you don't know it. Well, it's reopened. And do you know what they're selling – the only thing they are selling as far as I could tell? Crows. Dead crows. Rows and rows and rows of hanging black crows. They're selling them – to eat, I think. (*Beat.*) Go and have a look if you like. Quite a sight.

Short pause. She comes and sits next to him, takes his hand, puts it on her stomach.

76

It's kicking. (*Her mind drifts away, to:*) You try and make sense. You start to ask yourself – should I do this? Should I do that? (*Beat.*) You have such a wonderful smell about you. (*She takes his hand and holds it.*) We're all alone. (*Pause. She suddenly stands.*) I need to go for a pee. Excuse me.

> *She goes off down the hallway to the bedrooms and WC.*
> *Peter is alone. He sits, nearly frozen.*
> *Ann returns, tying her dressing gown.*

Walking past your room, I noticed you haven't made your bed, Peter. (*Beat.*) If you'd like, I could make it. (*Beat.*) Could I make it? (*Beat.*) I'll go and make your bed, Peter.

> *She goes off down the hallway to his bedroom. Peter watches her go, stands, and follows her out.*

SCENE SEVEN

Early evening.
> *Peter sits on the sofa, his book in his lap.*
> *There is a knock on the door. Peter does not respond. Another knock.*

Vi (*off*) Is that the door? Peter, will you get it?!

> *Peter does not move. Another knock.*

Peter?!

> *Another knock. Vi hurries on from the bedrooms.*

Did you hear the door?!

> *Suddenly it is like Peter 'comes to' – he really hadn't heard it.*
> *Vi opens the door, and there is Hugh, flowers in hand.*

Hugh May I come in?

Vi Please, of course. Betty will be – Shall I take those? (*The flowers.*)

Hugh (*joking*) They're not for you.

Vi (*embarrassed*) I know. I meant –

Hugh laughs a little too loudly.

Hugh And where is that beautiful sister of yours –?

Vi She'll be out in –

Ann, dressed now, appears in the kitchen doorway.

Hugh (*seeing Ann and pointing*) There she is! (*He laughs.*)

Ann Peter, get Hugh a drink. He's a man in need of a drink. You remember Peter.

Hugh (*over this*) I'm teasing.

Vi I'll tell Betty you're here.

She goes. Peter has got up and goes to the drinks.

Hugh (*as if explaining, to Peter*) I have four sisters. (*He smiles.*)

Peter Whisky?

Hugh (*nods, then*) Where's Mike –? Is he –?

Ann Not home yet. Any minute, I suppose.

Hugh (*looking at his watch*) I'm impressed. He's working –

Anne Let me get you something to have with your drink.

She goes into the kitchen, leaving Peter and Hugh alone. Peter hands Hugh his drink.

Hugh (*sips, then nods towards where Ann exited*) When's the baby – due?

Peter I don't know. (*Short pause. Peter sits back on the sofa.*)

Hugh He'll be a wonderful father.

Peter Good.

Hugh With some men – you can't tell. Me – I did my best. You saw my best. But it's a winnerless race raising a child. As I used to tell my ex-wife – the goal seems to be . . . to cause the least harm you can. (*Sips.*) He's a good man. Mike. Much admired. I understand he pays for all this –

Peter I know.

Hugh Everything. (*Beat.*) And now you too. Ann's a lucky woman.

Peter And you're a lucky man.

This confuses Hugh. He half smiles.

Hugh How so?

Peter Betty. She's the smartest of all us –

Hugh (*seriously*) It's a date. (*Shrugs.*) Don't make too much out of it. You understand, I'm sure.

Beat.

Peter (*continuing*) The smartest, cleverest. She was the only one of us who was ever able to finish anything. She finished school. I'm sure she's a great nurse –

Hugh But what about those ankles? (*He smiles.*)

Peter (*erupting*) For Christ's sake – she's not a piece of meat!

79

Hugh I'm teasing. I'm teasing you, Peter. If we can't take a joke any more . . . I told you – four sisters. (*Beat.*) Sorry.

Ann comes out with a tray with biscuits.

Ann What were you two –?

Peter Hugh has four sisters.

Ann My condolences. And how is your lovely daughter?

She turns to Peter for help.

Peter Rose.

Ann Rose. I love that name.

Peter (*to Hugh*) She wasn't scarred by the divorce?

Both Hugh and Ann are surprised by the question.

By your wife leaving you – for that American? The one you found in your wife's bed? (*Beat. Smiles.*) I'm just teasing.

Hugh Ask her. (*To Ann.*) Boys love her, as you can guess.

Peter Was your divorce difficult? I suppose what I'm really asking is – was it expensive?

He glances at Ann, then back to Hugh.

Hugh Not terribly. We decided most things before even talking to a solicitor.

Peter And that made it – less expensive?

Hugh Yes.

Peter again looks at Ann. Vi bursts in.

Vi Hugh, here she comes!

Betty enters in her mother's blue dress, hem raised to the knee, looking great. No one says anything for a moment, then:

Hugh You look great.

Nervous laughter.

Betty (*seeing the flowers*) Are those for me?

She takes them, kisses Hugh on the cheek.

Thank you. (*To Vi.*) Would you put them in water for me?

Vi takes the flowers.

(*To Hugh.*) Where are you taking me?

Hugh (*shrugs, then*) A drink first at the corner at the King's Head? Then – dinner?

Betty (*making a joke*) At the King's Head?!

Hugh No, no I didn't mean –

Betty Sounds like fun. And then – after – we'll see.

The sisters react to this boldness: 'Ohhh!' Hugh laughs nervously. Peter just watches.

Hugh I like this girl!

Betty (*holding up her jumper, to Hugh*) Would you mind?

Hugh helps her on with her jumper.

Should we go? Or do you want to finish that –? (*The drink.*)

Hugh swallows the rest.

(*To Vi.*) Goodnight. (*Kisses Vi.*) Goodnight, Ann. And baby. (*Kisses Ann.*) Goodnight. (*Kisses Peter.*)

Hugh Don't worry, she's in good hands. (*Laughs.*)

Peter Is that a joke too?

Vi (*over this, 'suddenly serious'*) Betty!

Betty What?

Vi quickly lifts up Betty's dress a bit. Betty, confused, pushes her hand away.

Vi Just making sure you're all dressed.

She laughs. Betty smiles at the joke. Everyone is saying 'Goodnight', 'Have a nice time', etc. The door is closed, they are gone, and immediately all the smiles disappear.

Peter Am I mad or did she look just like Mother?

Ann Just like her.

Vi nods. Pause. No one knows what to do. Ann starts rubbing her hands together.

Vi Are you all right?

Ann I'm fine –

Vi Your hands are freezing.

Ann I'll just put another jumper on. (*She starts to go.*)

Peter (*to Ann*). That was interesting what he said about getting a divorce. It doesn't have to cost – everything.

Ann goes. Vi is confused by this, then turns to Peter.

Vi What a woman goes through to have a baby.

Peter Is that why she's –?

Vi I watch Ann and I think – never me. What about you? You want children?

Peter I haven't thought about it.

Vi Men don't, I find. Of course they have less reason to. Or need to – think about it. (*Beat.*) I loaned Betty a couple of French letters. She's a virgin, did you know that? Why would you? A virgin. She just told me. I couldn't believe it. I had to show her how to put them on. (*Holds up her finger and demonstrates.*) To make sure it was tight . . . You . . . (*Stops.*) You don't want to know about this. (*Beat.*) Twenty-one years old and still a . . . I asked her – why? There must be some reason she's had for waiting. Some – principle? Belief? No, she said. There was no reason.

Beat.

Peter So – Hugh??

Vi (*shrugs*) She said – she wondered if it was finally time to grow up.

Peter Grow up? Is that growing up? Is – Hugh –?

Ann enters with another jumper.

Ann (*entering*) What are we doing for supper? Anything?

Vi Shhh! We're in the middle of a very interesting conversation. (*She turns to Peter.*) Are you a virgin, Peter?

Ann Vi, you can't just ask –

Vi (*over this*) If he doesn't want to answer, he doesn't have to.

Beat.

Peter No, no, I'm not a virgin.

Ann I think I'll go and begin a supper.

She goes.

Vi She has no curiosity. (*Calls.*) If you need any help, just . . . (*Beat.*) She can't hear me. What about a drink? I need a drink.

She gets up and goes to the drinks, stops.

We should have asked if she (*Ann*) was a virgin.

She laughs. Peter smiles.

'Let me get you a drink, Father.' (*As she makes drinks.*) That's what Mother always said. 'Let me get –' Explain something to me, why would a woman call her husband 'Father'? (*Beat.*) What did you do today?

Peter Nothing.

Vi (*not listening, handing him his drink*) 'Father'! Cheers. You spent all day here with Ann?

Peter Yes.

Vi Then you deserve that drink. Betty didn't even know how to put one on and she's a nurse! You look different today. Why do you look different?

No response.

You must have got some sleep. (*Beat.*) I got the part in *Autumn Fire*. The director changed his mind.

Peter Congratulations.

Vi (*over this*) That's good, isn't it? I'll have to be away for a while. On my own. You're the first to know.

Peter Vi, I love Ann.

Vi So do I. (*Beat.*) We're your sisters. You have to! (*Smiles.*) Not that it's always been – (*Touching her forehead.*) I was looking in the mirror earlier, see this? (*Points to a spot on her forehead.*) See this little mark? You know how I got that? You, Petey –

Peter Don't call me –

Vi You hit me with a stone. I was maybe – four? Do you remember this?

Peter shakes his head.

Why should you. (*Beat.*) The scars we leave. (*She sits back.*) The first time I had sex – Does this embarrass you?

Peter shakes his head.

Good. I was fifteen. He was a boy. Also from London. He hadn't seen his parents for – years too. We hung around. We played. When Ann wouldn't let me play with her friends. (*Beat.*) We did it outside. In the woods. I didn't have anything. No one told me about French letters. At least not how to get one. We both were pretty frightened. He was younger than me. Same as you. You'd like him, I think. I don't know where he is now. (*Beat.*) Then that afternoon – when I got back to the house from the woods? A telegram was waiting for us. To tell us that Mother had died. (*Beat.*) Guilty? Did I feel guilty, Peter? The scars we leave. (*Beat.*) There is no greater curse on a child, I believe, than to tie together once and for ever – sex and death.

Pause.

Peter I mean – I love Ann as a woman.

Vi turns to him.

I love her body. I love to touch –

Vi suddenly slaps him hard across the face. He nearly falls over.

Vi Stop it! Stop it!! That's disgusting!

Ann enters from the kitchen.

85

Ann What – ?!

Vi (*making a 'joke'*) He got fresh. (*She tries to laugh.*)

Peter (*trying to lie*) I hit my head against . . .

He looks to find something he could have hit his head against.

Ann Against what?

Peter The sofa. The side of the sofa.

Ann How did you –?

Peter I was leaning and I –?

Ann Why were you leaning?

Peter I just hit it. That's all. I'm not sure how it happened. It was one of those – things.

Ann goes to him and looks at the bruise. She touches his face. Vi watches.

Vi Is the supper . . .?

Ann It needs to cook.

She continues to touch Peter's face.

Peter I'm all right. I really am.

Vi Leave him alone.

Ann What?? (*She lets go of Peter.*)

Vi Leave our brother alone. He's not a child. We don't have to keep fawning over him.

They look at each other, then Vi turns away.

(*Turning away.*) Leave him alone. What were we talking about? The day Mother died. I was just talking about the day Mother died. I walk out of the woods, a little bloody, and Mum's dead. We're not the sisters you left. Are we, Ann? So much happened. There's so much Peter doesn't know about. So much he's missed. (*Beat.*) There was that woman. Weeks, months later? After Mother's death, Father comes to visit us – with a woman. What was her name?

No response from Ann.

We never wrote to you about any of this. And the most remarkable thing was that she looked like Mother. Like a rather blurry carbon copy of Mother. Wouldn't you agree?

Ann Exactly.

Peter looks at Ann.

Vi We look at her – we didn't know what to say. Father's got his arm around her. They hold hands. What am I to feel? Do I love her? Do I hate her? She tried – to be nice. At supper that night she was very nice. Then we went for a walk in the morning. Just 'us girls'. (*Beat.*) And we learned, didn't we, that she was obsessed with Mother. With things she'd heard – been told –

Ann That Father was telling her –

Vi Lies. How Mother had been so mean with some things –

Ann Books, he told her.

Peter Mother was never mean with books –

Vi (*over this*) And positively extravagant when it came to other things – for herself. Shoes. How many shoes? That was not true! He was lying to her about Mother! Mother bought maybe three pairs of shoes at one time only because she had such narrow feet that when she found shoes that fitted her – which was rare! – she bought a few pairs! That makes sense. Doesn't it make sense?! That doesn't make her a spendthrift. That doesn't make her selfish, for God's sake! She kept every damn shoe she ever bought and dyed them over and over and over! This wasn't our mother, woman! I know it sounds petty, but I can still see that face, that almost-mother's face, how I wanted to slap that face as she said, I remember every word, as she took my hand on that walk and said: 'It seems your mother wasn't a very kind woman. How hard that must have been for you. Still, I'm sure she tried to love you in her own way.' (*Short pause.*) We're weak, Peter. We've become very weak. (*To Ann.*) Leave him alone.

Ann looks to Peter.

Peter I told her. She knows.

Ann nods. Peter turns to her, leans and kisses her on the mouth and fondles her breast. She lets him.

Vi (*covering her ears and closing her eyes, shouts*) No!!!

Silence.

Ann What else has he missed about our family, Vi? There's the letters. (*To Peter.*) Why didn't he burn them? He was off to war, for God's sake! Letters to Father from women. Over years and years. (*Beat.*) Mother must have known.

Vi We disagree about that.

Ann I've read them. Vi's read them. Betty's so far refused. Just say when. (*She takes Peter's hand in hers.*)

Vi This is wrong. I hurt so much. (*Holds herself and whimpers.*) No. No. No.

Short pause.

Peter (*to Ann*) Vi got that part in that play. The director changed his mind.

Ann Good for you, Vi.

Vi I went to see the director today. At his flat. And slept with him. (*Beat. As a second thought.*) The girl without – (*Gestures.*) And her legs crossed? She had had the role.

Short pause.

Ann As Vi said – we're not the sisters you left.

Short pause.

Peter So poor Vi will have to be away from home for a while.

Short pause.

Ann Mike's looking at a new flat, Vi – for the baby. So I could be away from home too.

Door opens, Betty enters.

(*Letting go of Peter's hand.*) Betty, why are you –?

Vi (*same time*) Where's Hugh?

Betty looks at them and smiles. She is suddenly calm, not at all the flighty person she has been.

Betty I don't know. I just – left. I don't know what happened – it was like someone spoke to me and said: 'Look at this man, Betty. Have you looked at him?' (*Beat.*) So I did. And I saw – a nose I disliked. Talk about thick ankles – look at his nose. And hands – with all those hairs. And I hate his laugh. I hate his teasing. So why am I here? (*Beat.*) This isn't me. So I said I didn't feel well and came home. (*Turns to Ann.*) Ann, could you put the kettle on, please?

Vi I'll do it –

Betty Let Ann. She's always telling us not to wait on her.

Vi When has she said –?

Betty Shhh.

Ann (*getting up*) I'll put the kettle on. (*She goes.*)

Betty In the pub, Hugh got quite close to me and said, 'I hope this isn't difficult for you, but I've asked Mike to join us for dinner. I think he's bringing his other nurse.'

Ann returns.

Ann Kettle's on. (*Beat.*) We'll eat when Mike's home.

Betty (*picking up a framed photo*) I think it was Mother who spoke to me. Her voice. That's what I'm going to believe. Now I'm going to get out of her dress and give it back to her.

She goes down the hallway to the bedrooms. Ann looks at Peter.

Vi Leave him alone.

Beat.

Ann I should keep an eye on the stew.

She hesitates, goes to Peter, squeezes his shoulder, then leaves for the kitchen.
Vi has picked up the photo Betty had held. She sets it back down.
Peter starts to stand, to follow Ann, when:

Vi Stay in here.

Peter sits back down. Beat.

The ship after yours – the next ship carrying boys and girls to Canada – was torpedoed by the Germans and sank.

Peter I know that.

Vi (*ignoring him*) They wouldn't let anyone – go after that. You were the last. (*Beat.*) We waited a full week wondering what had happened. If it had been your ship. (*Beat.*) We thought then we might have lost you. I even imagined, sitting in the bath, what it would have been like, felt like – to drown. And to float to the bottom of the sea. Like a leaf, I thought, as it falls. We cried ourselves to sleep. (*Beat.*) The first newspaper accounts said that the little boys had stood in perfect lines, all straight, all calm. Some could get into boats, some couldn't. Calm. Betty said that surely meant you couldn't be on that ship, our little Peter couldn't ever stand still. (*She smiles at Peter, then:*) For a week we held our breath. And then we heard. You were in Canada. You were lucky. How we celebrated! Mum and Dad and Betty and Ann and me. How happy we were that our Peter was safe. I'd never known a happier day. (*She picks up the photo again.*) I began to dream you were coming home. (*Beat.*) Then, finally, you really were coming home. (*She sets the photo back down.*) Now you're home. (*She stands. Calls.*) Betty, I'll help you with that dress!

> She heads down the hallway. Peter sits alone on the sofa.
> Suddenly, from far off, the distant cry of a baby.
> The cry gets louder and louder, closer and closer.
> The baby is screaming now.
> Peter doesn't move, doesn't flinch as the baby screams.

SCENE EIGHT

Months later. Midnight.

The room is dark. Outside, in the hallway, a baby is crying.

Someone is trying to unlock the door. Finally, it opens and Mike and Ann enter. She carries their crying infant.

Ann (*rocking*) Shh. They're not up. They're asleep. Maybe we should –

Mike They won't be for long. (*He nods down the hall to the bedrooms.*) Someone's turned on a light.

Ann (*rocking*) Shh. Turn on a lamp.

Mike turns on a lamp. There is a cup and saucer on a table.

Look at this mess. These children need a mother.

Mike It's a cup and saucer.

Betty, tying her dressing gown, enters from the bedrooms.

Betty Ann? Is that you? What are you –?

Vi (*right behind her*) They brought Mary!

The aunts go to the child.

Betty What's wrong? Is something wrong?

Ann Shh. Shh.

Mike Colic. I tell her it'll pass. She's worried –

Ann I'm not worried.

Mike (*over this*) And I'm also her doctor! Give her to them. Give her . . . Look at your sisters, they're drooling to – They won't drop her –

Ann begins handing over the baby to Betty.

Betty Shh. Shh. She's so sweet.

Vi What time is it?

Mike Midnight.

Vi What are you doing –?

Mike (*to Betty*) We miss you at the surgery.

Betty (*just rocks the baby, ignoring Mike*) God, I love her.

Peter appears in the doorway to Mike and Ann's old bedroom (now his). He has thrown on trousers, and is buttoning his shirt. He is barefoot.

Peter What is – all this?

Mike Peter! (*To Ann.*) He is here. You weren't sure –

Peter Sure what?

Vi Ann's brought Mary.

Mike I'll wager he guessed that.

Peter (*about the crying*) What's wrong?

Ann It's nothing – colic. It goes away. It's a phase, Mike says.

Betty Maybe she needs to be changed.

Ann You can try that, sometimes –

Vi Or she's hungry.

Ann I just fed her.

Mike We brought nappies –

Betty Let's take her into our room and change her on the bed. (*To Ann.*) Do you mind?

93

Ann I'll have my chances. Please. I hold her enough.

Vi (*to Betty*) Why don't you let me –

Ann Please, don't fight over her.

Smiles. Vi takes the still-crying baby.
As the baby is taken out of the room Mike sits on the sofa and sighs:

Mike The lungs on that child. I am so tired.

Soon he will fall asleep sitting up. Ann and Peter look at each other.

Ann I thought you might want to see your niece. You can go – if you want –

Peter She's beautiful. I'll see more of her later. She's very beautiful.

Big yawn from Mike.

Mike Children . . .

Ann It's not too late –?

Peter No.

Ann You were up?

Peter Yes.

Beat.

Ann You didn't come to the hospital. I don't blame you, they're . . . (*Beat. Looks around.*) Our first time out. We just brought her home, you know. She was crying. We couldn't sleep.

She looks at Mike, who is falling asleep.

I couldn't sleep. (*Smiles.*) So I thought to myself – where can we go? Who'd take us in? (*Smiles again.*) And I

knew you'd be anxious to see her. To meet your niece.
I thought you'd been waiting – It's great to see you.

They look at each other. He reaches for her hand. She resists.

You deserve better than me. You're my brother.

Suddenly, young Rose, Hugh's daughter, comes out from Peter's bedroom, wearing Peter's dressing gown.

Rose Peter? What's going on? Why is that baby crying?

Ann is stunned to see Rose.

Peter Go back to bed. They'll be gone soon.

Rose Is the baby all right? It's not sick –

Ann She's fine. They're changing her.

Rose Could I watch? I love babies.

Ann Put some clothes on first.

Rose (*in disbelief*) What?

Ann I said, young lady, put some clothes on first.

Rose looks at Peter, hesitates, then hurries back to put on clothes.

Was that who I think it was?

Peter Rose.

Ann Thank you, I forgot the name. God, you people keep secrets.

Peter We just went out for the first time tonight.

Ann I see. (*Beat.*) Good for you. Good for you.

She goes to hug Peter. He hesitates, then allows himself to be hugged.

95

Though I hope you don't get serious about her. You can do better than that. After all, you're my brother.

This makes Peter smile. Ann sits in a chair. Mike is sound asleep.

It's breezy outside. She'll probably catch a cold. (*Beat.*) What kind of mother am I?

She turns to Peter for comfort or a compliment.

Peter I don't know.

Short pause.

Ann When I was in labour, when I was . . . out – Mike made sure I was out – I had a dream about the baby. I dreamed my baby and I were taking a trip together. Just us. Her and me. We were climbing mountains somewhere. Maybe – Canada? Your mountains?

Peter They're not my –

Ann The sky was so blue. Her face young and happy. And then suddenly she slipped, Peter, and she started to fall. I reached down and grabbed her hand. I was the only thing keeping her from death. (*Beat.*) She was dangling over the side of a cliff, my hand gripping her wrist. She was so heavy, Peter. I thought my whole arm would fall off. But I held on. (*Beat.*) Then somehow I found the strength, the power inside me, a power that surprised me, that I never knew I possessed, and I pulled my baby to safety. I saved her, Peter. (*Beat.*) I saved her. (*Beat.*) And then there she was again – a baby in my arms. (*Beat.*) You'll adore her. And she'll worship you.

The crying has stopped.

She's stopped crying.

Vi appears.

Vi (*in a loud whisper*) If you sing to her, she stops crying!

Vi hurries back to the baby. Off, we hear Vi and Betty singing. Ann and Peter listen.

Peter What are they singing?

They and we begin to make out the song: 'Goodnight Children Everywhere'.

Vi *and* **Betty** (*off*)
She's with you night and day
Goodnight children, everywhere.

Mike snores.
Peter and Ann don't move, can't move, they only listen.

Sleepy little eyes and sleepy little head
Sleepy time is drawing near.
In a little while
You'll be tucked up in your bed
Here's a song for baby dear.

Fighting back tears, and without looking at each other, Peter snaps his fingers once – because he is thinking of Mother.
Ann snaps her fingers once.
Then after a moment, Ann snaps her fingers twice – she is thinking of Father.
Peter snaps his fingers twice. The singing continues.
Rose bursts in, buttoning her blouse. She crosses the room and exits to go and see the baby. Neither seems to notice her. Off:

Goodnight children, everywhere
Your mummy thinks of you tonight,
Lay your head upon your pillow,
Don't be a kid or a weeping willow.

Close your eyes and say a prayer
And surely you can find a kiss to spare.
Though you are far away
She's with you night and day
Goodnight children, everywhere.

FRANNY'S WAY

I believe I essentially remain what I've almost
always been – a narrator, but one with extremely
pressing personal needs.

J. D. Salinger
Seymour: An Introduction

Franny's Way was first performed by Playwrights Horizons on 6 March 2002. The cast was as follows:

Older Franny / Grandma Kathleen Widdoes
Young Franny Elisabeth Moss
Dolly Domenica Cameron-Scorsese
Sally Yvonne Woods
Phil Jesse Pennington

Director Richard Nelson
Set design Thomas Lynch
Costume design Susan Hilferty and Linda Ross
Lighting design Jennifer Tipton
Sound design Scott Lehrer

The play was subsequently performed at the Geffen Playhouse, opening on 28 June 2003. The cast was as follows:

Older Franny / Grandma Penny Fuller
Young Franny Elisabeth Moss
Dolly Domenica Cameron-Scorsese
Sally Susan May Pratt
Phil Jesse Pennington

Director Richard Nelson
Set design Thomas Lynch
Costume design Susan Hilferty
Lighting design David Weiner
Sound design Scott Lehrer

Characters

Franny
seventeen

Dolly
her sister, fifteen

Sally
their cousin, twenties

Phil
Sally's husband, twenties

Grandma (Marjorie)
Franny, Dolly and Sally's grandmother

Older Franny
(also plays Grandma)

An apartment, Sullivan Street,
Greenwich Village, 1957

For Tim Sanford

Lights up on a tenement apartment, Sullivan Street,
Greenwich Village, 1957. Living room and kitchen are
combined: chairs, kitchen table, refrigerator, counter,
sofa, etc. Doors to two small bedrooms, one closed, one
open. A door to the hallway. The bathroom is in the
hallway and shared.

   An open window through which we hear the sounds
of Sullivan Street – traffic, voices, and those of Bleecker
around the corner. Distant jazz from a club – mostly
horns, something like Miles Davis's Sketches of Spain.
Except for what comes from the window, the only light
comes from the open bedroom and it is very dim.

   Late night. Late June. It is hot.

   Slowly we begin to hear noises from the closed
bedroom, a groan, a cry. A couple are making love.
They reach a climax and the woman shouts out.

   Pause.

   Bedroom door opens. A young man, Phil, comes out.
He is naked. In the bedroom, a young woman, Sally, sits
on the edge of the bed, also naked. They are in their
twenties and married.

   Phil, wiping the sweat off his face, then on to some
furniture as he passes, heads for the refrigerator. He
opens the door – light – and takes out a bottle of beer.
He opens it and drinks as he looks out of the window.
The jazz in the distance.

   He breathes heavily, catching his breath; he goes and
turns on an electric fan. Sally comes into the room. As
Phil is turning on the fan:

Phil (*holding up his beer*) You want a –(*sip*)?

Sally Shh. Shh.

And she gestures toward the other bedroom. They listen for an instant, then relax, smile, even a little giggle as if they have gotten away with something. She nods, and goes to light a cigarette. He hands her the bottle, she takes a big sip, and they both end up looking out of the window. He sits with her on the sofa and holds her, kisses her neck. She responds. Sips again, smokes. They listen to the music. She moves to it a bit.

Sally (*after a deep sigh*) God, is it hot. There's no air out there. (*Looks at the fan.*) Does that reach –? I can't feel anything.

Phil Let me try.

As he stands, a metal object – a baby's rattle – falls on the floor. The noise makes the couple suddenly stop and turn to the open bedroom, expecting to hear something now. There is silence. This at first makes them smile, and Sally takes another sip or drag, but then she stops, looks concerned at Phil and heads for this bedroom.

Shh. Don't –

Sally I won't.

She goes into the bedroom. Phil plays with the rattle.

(*In the bedroom.*) Phil? Phil? (*Louder.*) Phil!! Come here!

Phil (*hurrying to the bedroom*) Sally? What's –? (*He turns on the bedroom light – bright light.*)

Sally (*at the same time*) Anna? Anna!!

She is nearly screaming now. In the bedroom, she holds up a baby. Screams.

Phil!!

Sally begins to cry and scream. Phil tries to take Anna from her, but she pushes him away.

What's wrong with Anna? Something's wrong. Phil!

Phil Don't shake her! Anna?

Sally Phil, she's blue!

Phil Wake up, wake up.

Sally Make her wake up! Please, help her, Phil. Help her!

He runs out of the bedroom into their bedroom. He comes out trying to put on his trousers. The jazz continues from Bleecker Street.

Phil Oh God, Jesus, Anna, please, please.

Sally Sweetie. Wake up, dear. Open your eyes. Mommy's here. Mommy's here. Wake up. Phil!

Phil (*screams*) Sally!!

Lights fade out

SCENE ONE

The Older Franny speaks to the audience.

Older Franny Cousin Sally's and her husband's baby was already dead when they found her in her bed. 'Crib death' was what was written on the death certificate. Father said 'Who the hell knows why?' would have been just as appropriate.

I was seventeen. This death, which swept as a tidal wave over the lives of Sally and Phil, was by the time it

reached my distant shore – in Millbrook, New York –
but a small almost unnoticed ripple. Perhaps I sent a
condolence card. Or maybe I spoke to her briefly during
one of her calls with Grandma. Or perhaps it was merely
a 'poor Sally' thought I had, which never even got
expressed.

I had, after all, other things on my mind that summer.
There was a boyfriend, with whom I had had my first
sex, and he was now at NYU. And I loved him. Though
his letters were beginning to get, if not less frequent, then
less – interesting. Was this my fault? Or his? I was in the
midst of my novel about the rivalries between five sisters
in Victorian Yorkshire England which consumed my
summer afternoons. There was my new stepmother.
I thought about her a lot. My mother I think I was
adamantly choosing not to think about. So that took
some time too. And then there was my name, my new
chosen, changed name. Changed from the matronly and
phoney 'Frances' to – Franny. My homage, I liked to
call it, to the beautiful, frail, lost, fair-skinned, funny,
faint-prone heroine of my life and J.D. Salinger's story.
I saw myself navigating my way through life's sea of
phonies. I was missing only her raccoon coat, but it was
still summer – and my birthday was coming up. Anyway,
as I said, I had a lot to think about.

So when Grandma offered to take my sister and me on
a trip to New York City, it simply didn't occur to me
that our purpose was to console my grieving cousin, but
rather seemed the very understandable fulfilment of a
seventeen-year-old's desire, if not need, to get the hell out
of Millbrook and be hurtled headlong into that swirl of
life called New York.

My little sister, too, had her own plans for this trip.

We took the two-hour train trip from Dover Plains to
Grand Central, and climbed down into the subway and
back up again downtown, up into the noise and music of

the Village. We then walked down Bleecker with its clubs, doors left open because of the summer's heat, their sounds like breaths, puffs, exhaled into the street, into clouds of music we walked through, until we got here, on Sullivan, in the heart of Greenwich Village, which for my money and in my dreams was the very soul and centre of the whole goddamn universe.

So it was on a Tuesday night, in August 1957, barely six weeks after the baby, Anna's, tragic and inexplicable, and by me nearly forgotten death, that my sister, age fifteen –

Dolly enters from the hallway, small suitcase in hand.

And me, age seventeen –

Seventeen-year-old Franny enters, looking around excitedly. She too carries a small bag. Phil has come in with them, holding a larger suitcase.

And our grandma – she was about the same age then as I am now, so I'll be her – arrived, ready to spend two exciting and unforgettable days – of real life. (*Older Franny will play the Grandma throughout.*)

August 1957. Eleven p.m. Jazz, though much more percussive than before, is now heard through the window, as well as the sound and noises of the street. Sally has come out of her bedroom and is greeting everyone. Everyone is speaking at once.

Sally (*to Dolly*) Look at you. Who let you grow up?! (*Laughs.*)

Franny Where should we put –(*her bag*)?

Phil Anywhere.

Sally (*over this, continuing to Dolly*) Does your father know how much you've grown up?

Grandma He sees her every day.

Sally I'm kidding her, Grandma. (*To Dolly, not letting go of the subject.*) I remember when you used to be –

Phil That's enough, Sally.

Sally Enough of what, I don't understand? What am I doing?

Awkward moment, then:

Grandma (*to Sally*) Oh dear, it's good to see you.

Sally (*pointing to Franny*) And you, I knew you'd grow up.

Franny (*to Phil*) What does that mean?

He shrugs.

Dolly Where's the bathroom?

Sally It's in the hall. We share –

Grandma (*looking around now*) What a nice apartment. (*It isn't.*) What's that music –?

Sally (*over-excited*) There's a jazz club. (*To Dolly as if to a child.*) You know what a jazz club is?

Franny (*to Grandma*) We passed it, Grandma.

Dolly (*to Phil*) The bathroom's in the hall?

Sally (*hearing this*) It's perfectly safe.

Franny I'll go with you.

Sally Does she need someone to –?

Phil They just got here, Sally. I'll get you a towel –

He moves towards their bedroom.

Sally I put towels on their bed.

Phil heads for the other bedroom.

Grandma Are we staying in – (*there*)? How lovely. (*She can barely conceal her disgust for the place.*)

Sally You and Dolly will share – Is that all right with –?

Dolly I heard. I've prepared myself.

Laughter.

Sally (*to Franny*) And you, it's either the couch, or we could put down a few cushions in the bedroom, if that would –

Franny I'll think about it.

Sally (*on to another subject*) Who's hungry? There's plenty of –

Dolly I have to use the –

Sally (*to Phil, who has a towel now*) Phil, show her –

Franny I'm going with her.

Franny takes the towel and goes out into the hall with Dolly. Awkward moment, Franny appears again.

Which door?

Phil The only one on the right.

Franny Do we knock or –?

Sally No one's in there. I was just in there.

Franny goes.

I can't believe how the little one's grown. (*To Grandma.*) Thank you for coming.

They hug.

Phil Yes, thank you, Marjorie. It's good to see you.

Sally (*to say something*) And Fran's a woman now –

Grandma Franny. We must now call her – Franny. She'll tell you why. (*To Phil.*) And how is work?

He nods.

You two are such a lovely couple.

No one knows what to say, then:

Sally Let me get you something to –

Grandma We had sandwiches on the train. I brought sandwiches. We hardly ate them. Are they excited! (*Beat.*) You won't believe what Dolly's done. You want to know what she and I are doing tomorrow?

Franny returns with Dolly behind her.

Franny (*in the doorway*) I think it's locked.

Sally No one was in there a minute ago. Philip, help them.

Franny I didn't want to push too hard.

Phil (*to Dolly, as they go out*) God, are you big!

Franny (*teasing*) What about me?

Phil You – you're still a kid and you always will be.

Tickling her, laughter, the door closes behind them. Short pause.

Sally They're young women. (*Starts to light a cigarette.*) I hope you'll be comfortable. It's not Millbrook.

A siren goes by outside.

You get used to the . . .

She looks around. Clearly Grandma does not know what to say. Then, pointing to the spare bedroom:

That was the baby's room. (*Suddenly changing the subject.*) What has Dolly . . .?

Grandma (*confused*) What?

Sally You were saying – Dolly's done some—

Grandma You won't believe it. You know she's never been to New York before –

Sally Really? I didn't know.

Grandma You couldn't believe how excited – 'Peel her off the roof!' That's what her father was saying this morning. We're seeing *My Fair Lady*.

Sally is confused.

That's what Dolly did. She organised – all by herself – tickets to . . . Her father paid for them of course – but she wrote off and – That's what we're doing tomorrow in the afternoon.

Sally That's exciting.

Grandma Aren't you proud of her? I couldn't have done that at her age. She wrote away and everything.

Phil returns.

Sally What was –?

Phil It was stuck. The toilet door. Franny is staying with her.

Grandma You remembered to call her Franny now –

Phil She told me.

Grandma Do you know that short story –?

Phil I do. (*Beat.*) And it's good. Marjorie, don't you want anything to –? (*Heads towards the kitchen area.*)

Sally I offered. They've eaten sandwiches. No one is hungry.

Phil What about something to drink? You must be –

Sally She doesn't want anything. I asked.

Grandma Actually, I am a little – (*thirsty*)

Phil (*to Sally*) Why didn't you offer –

Sally I did!

Phil You want a beer? There's Cokes, I'll bet the girls would like –

Sally I'll get them.

Phil (*over this*) I'll get them!

Pause as Phil goes to refrigerator and starts taking out Cokes.

(*The same safe subject.*) Dolly's gotten big, hasn't she?

Sally Like she all of a sudden sprang up. (*To Grandma.*) You probably don't notice it as –

Phil She notices it. (*Takes out glasses for the drinks.*)

Sally Maybe they don't want glasses. Kids like to drink from the bottle.

Phil We'll give them the choice then.

Short pause.

Grandma Dolly didn't take a sheep to the Dutchess County Fair this summer. So I suppose that's over.

Phil She's growing up.

Sally I used to take my sheep. I used to sleep with my sheep overnight. A lot of kids did. (*Beat.*) It was great.

Phil I'll bet.

Sally Bull. You hate the country. You hate animals. You hate –

Phil I don't hate animals.

Sally You think all farmers are –

Phil I do not.

Sally (*to Grandma*) He thinks our whole family are –

Phil I do not! (*Beat. To Grandma.*) I don't.

Sally (*changing the subject*) Dolly's never been to New York before. She and Grandma are seeing *My Fair Lady*.

Phil (*to Sally*) You wanted to see that.

Sally I'm jealous.

Phil (*moving towards the spare bedroom*) Franny says she wants to sleep in there. I'll set up the cushions –

Sally I'll do that.

Phil I don't mind.

Sally Which sheets are you going to –?

Phil Which sheets do you want me to use?

Sally (*exasperated*) I'll do it.

Phil I can make up a bed on a floor. I'm not that incompetent.

They look at each other.

Sally Go ahead then.

Grandma I can help if . . .

They ignore her. Phil goes into the bedroom. We see him through the open door as he makes up the bed. Sally goes to the refrigerator and starts taking a few things out.

Sally I made a few things . . .

Grandma Sally, it's after eleven. The kids should be going to bed. (*Pause.*) What did you make? (*Goes and looks over the dishes, turns to listen to music.*) Does that go on all night? The music.

Sally What music? (*Laughs a little too hard.*) That's a joke Phil and I . . . Yeah. It does.

Franny and Dolly return.

Dolly What a neat bathroom. I can't wait to take a bath in that tub.

Grandma Phil's making up your bed –

Sally So – *My Fair Lady.* Aren't you lucky. I'm jealous. (*Continues to set out food as she talks. To Dolly.*) I have a friend who auditioned for a replacement in that show. She was in my acting class with me.

Dolly Really?

Franny (*looking around*) This is so neat. Look at this.

She goes to the window. Dolly follows.

Sally Don't get too close to that –

Franny I'm not going to –

Sally I've told Phil a thousand times we need a bar, an iron bar, so no one . . . No child . . .

Franny I'm not a child.

Sally I didn't mean – Doesn't anyone want something to eat?!

This comes out almost as a cry, and we see that she is nearly in tears, trying not to cry.

I made things to eat.

Phil is in the doorway.

Phil (*impatient*) Sally.

Sally (*crying*) I'm trying not to!

Franny and Dolly are confused. They look to Grandma who begins to push them towards their bedroom.

Grandma You girls have a big day tomorrow –

Dolly Why is Sally –?

Phil (*as they approach him, heading for their bedroom, to Franny*) So, college! (*To the others.*) Franny says she's looking at colleges!

Grandma (*to Sally*) I didn't tell you, she's going to take a tour –

Phil (*teasing*) NYU!

Sally (*to Franny*) I didn't know. No one tells me –

Franny I have a friend who goes there. And – she wants me to look –

Phil And your father? Doesn't he know? He'd have a fit if you left Upstate – (*They are in the bedroom now.*) I can just hear him: 'We have excellent colleges up here, young lady.'

Dolly Sounds like Father.

Franny Except for the 'young lady' stuff. I've gotten him to stop that. I told him, 'Another "young lady", Dad, and this young lady is going to burn down one of your best barns.' I meant it too.

Phil, who obviously enjoys playing with these girls, goes 'Ohhh, that scared him'. Grandma goes and hugs Sally.

Sally I promised myself I wouldn't do that.

Another hug, then:

Grandma Your father wants you home. Both of you. He's got his eye on a nice house. I've seen it. (*Beat.*) Get away from here. And come home.

Sally (*wiping her tears*) I'm an actress, Grandma. I've got a new teacher. I know he'll take me. He's going to help me with my singing. That's what I need.

Phil comes out of the bedroom.

Phil Is it all right if Franny borrows a robe? She forgot hers.

Sally nods. Phil goes back into the bedroom. Sally gets a robe from their bedroom, returns.

Sally (*to Grandma*) He won't touch me, Grandma. He doesn't want me, since . . .

She tries not to cry. Grandma takes her hand, she pulls it away.

He hates me. And I hate him.

Grandma watches as Phil comes out of the bedroom to get the robe. Sally crosses and awkwardly hands him the robe.
He goes into the other bedroom, and suddenly Franny and Dolly attack him – they were hiding behind the door. Screams, laughter, etc., from this bedroom and the overexcited young women. The night sounds/music and lights begin to fade. Grandma shouts: 'Now get to bed. Phil, you're winding them up.'

SCENE TWO

*The middle of the night. The apartment is quiet, except
for soft music coming from the radio in Phil and Sally's
bedroom. No lights are on. No music from the club on
Bleecker Street, it is too late. A little noise from the
street.*

*Franny comes out of the bedroom, now in one of
Sally's robes. She is trying to make her way to the sink,
but is having trouble seeing; she kicks the leg of a chair
as she passes along the table.*

*At the sink, she turns on the tap, and drinks. She
notices the music coming from the bedroom. She slowly
heads to the window where she looks out, lost in thought.
A fire truck passes in the distance, voices from the street.
Franny watches.*

SCENE THREE

*Late the next morning. Light streams in from the
window. The noise from the street is alive and present –
people, crowds walking by, sirens, horns, etc.*

*Grandma is cleaning up after breakfast, still in her
nightgown. Dolly, dressed but a bit dishevelled – she
hasn't combed her hair yet, tucked in her blouse, etc. –
stands at the window. Sally, in a robe, sits at the table.*

Dolly (*looking out*) It's so interesting.

Grandma (*to Dolly*) It's not as much fun as it looks out
there.

Dolly I didn't say it was fun. I said it was really really
really interesting.

Sally It's that, Grandma. You can't argue with that.

Grandma Look at that. Look at what he's wearing. Oh my God.

Dolly It's summer –

Grandma (*going back to cleaning up, half to herself*) On a public street.

Pause. A church bell chimes in the distance.

Dolly She's still in there?

Grandma (*picks up the coffee pot*) Should I throw it out –?

Sally nods, then:

Sally No, I'll take it. I could go and knock . . .

Door to the hallway opens. Franny enters, dressed, combed, lost in her thoughts.

Here she is.

The others just look at Franny.

Franny What?? What's wrong? (*Starts to fix her hair.*) Why are you looking at me?

Sally Nothing.

Dolly Phil had to shave in the kitchen sink.

Franny What?? Why did he do that?

Grandma He shaved in the –?

Dolly You were still in the bedroom, Grandma. (*To Franny.*) He had to get to work. He works.

Sally Dolly –

Franny What does that have to do with me?

Dolly You've been hogging the bathroom, Franny. How long was she in the –?

Franny Why didn't he knock?

Dolly *Everyone*'s been waiting to use the bathroom –

Franny Why didn't anyone knock –?

Grandma There's just the one bathroom – and it's not just for us, but for the whole floor. Isn't that right? It's not like home, Franny.

Franny But why –?

Sally It's fine. Leave her alone. Philip didn't mind. (*To Grandma.*) It'll give him something to talk about.

Franny There's nothing for him to talk about! Jesus. What did I do? I don't understand.

Dolly She always hogs the bathroom. She doesn't think about anyone else needing to use the –

Franny (*to Dolly*) Shut up.

Grandma Girls –

Dolly I've been in there with her. She'll stare at herself in the mirror for –

Franny Leave me alone! (*Looks at her sister.*) What are you talking about? Do you know what you're talking about? Maybe if you took a bath a little more often, you wouldn't have to slap so much deodorant on.

Grandma Franny –

Franny You think no one can smell it? It's true. Smell her. Go ahead. (*To Sally.*) You don't have to sleep in the same room as –

Grandma (*to Dolly*) I didn't smell –

Franny You can't smell anything, Grandma.

Short pause. Dolly turns back and looks out of the window.

Bathroom's free.

She turns to go into the bedroom. Dolly laughs under her breath, Franny turns back.

Why don't you jump?

Grandma Maybe I should get dressed.

Franny (*to Dolly*) Or maybe you need a push –

She hurries to Dolly. Sally grabs Franny.

Sally Stop it! Stop.

Franny (*same time*) I wasn't going to –

Sally How old are you two anyway?!

Dolly suddenly musses up Franny's hair and runs for cover.

Franny Damn you!

Sally Don't swear –

Franny (*over this*) What are you –? I just fixed . . . (*Tries to fix her hair.*) I'll kill you.

Grandma Who wants to use the bathroom next?

Dolly (*all of her focus still on Franny*) Sorry to mess up your hair for your big – 'appointment'.

Franny You shut up, Dolly.

Grandma (*suddenly*) What big appointment?

Franny doesn't know what to say.

Franny (*under her breath to Dolly*) You are in big trouble.

Dolly Me? Really?

Grandma I thought you were just going to walk around the campus with your friend. Do you have an appointment at the college?

Franny No, Grandma. I don't know what my little sister is talking about. But that is usually the case, isn't it? We must all be used to that by now. I should go. Betty's probably waiting for me.

Dolly 'Betty'?

Franny (*to Sally*) Betty's a friend from home. She goes to NYU. She promised to show me around. (*Trying hard.*) Of course Father says there's a million good schools upstate or in New England, why in the world would a girl want to live in New York City when . . . when there's all that there, I suppose. (*Looks at Sally.*) Betty's two years older. Very responsible. I'll be fine, don't worry. Is my hair –?

Dolly Oh God, don't let her go back into the bathroom!

Franny (*suddenly turns on Dolly*) And – Dolly, what are your 'big' plans for today?

This stops Dolly. She looks at her sister, then:

Dolly We're seeing the play. She (*Sally*) knows that.

Sally I'm so proud of you for sending off and getting tickets all by yourself.

Franny She's not five years old, Sally. Far from it.

Starts for the bedroom, then stops.

Oh, you're just 'seeing the play'. I see. Careful, sister. Now you leave me alone.

She goes into their bedroom.

Sally (*suddenly standing*) We should all get dressed.

Dolly (*at the same time*) Grandma, we should go –

Grandma Mind if I use the . . . bathroom?

Sally (*to Dolly*) You've got loads of time. A matinee's not until two thirty –

Dolly We're going to Gimbels first.

Grandma She wants to go to Gimbels.

Dolly Get ready, Grandma.

Grandma There's something there she's been looking for. At Gimbels. She won't tell me what it is. It's a big secret.

Smiles, even winks at Dolly, and, picking up a pile of clothes she is going to wear, heads into the hallway to the bathroom. Pause. Dolly goes back to looking out of the window. Sally looks at Dolly. Then, to say something:

Sally So – you like shows too.

Dolly nods.

I love them.

Dolly smiles.

How's your father? Surviving okay?

Dolly Sure.

Sally doesn't know whether to say more, then:

Sally I really like your father. A shame about what your mother did to him –

Dolly (*interrupting – she doesn't want to talk about it*) He's just fine. Really.

Sally My dad thinks the world of him. Of his 'little brother'. Funny to think about it that way, isn't it? His little . . . Dad says your father's going through a lot, but who'd know? That's what he says. (*Beat.*) You should have seen the letter your father wrote me after our baby . . . After what happened –

Dolly suddenly turns from the window.

Dolly Oh my God, Sally, I'm so sorry, I haven't said how sorry I am for what –

Sally I wasn't asking for –

Dolly (*same time*) No, I know, but –

Sally I didn't mean to – I know your feelings. You don't have to . . . It's probably better that you haven't said anything. Let it all – heal.

Dolly is still kicking herself for not saying anything.

You don't want to just keep – picking at it. Then it'll never get better. So . . . Don't worry, I wasn't expecting . . .

Dolly I am sorry –

Sally And you guys are just kids.

Franny (*entering, all dressed, shoes, etc., carrying her purse*) Who's a kid? Don't include me in –

Dolly (*as soon as she sees Franny*) Sally was just talking about her baby.

It hits Franny too.

Franny Oh God. Sally, I'm so sorry –

Dolly (*over this*) She doesn't want – She isn't asking –

Franny I wrote you, didn't I? I was planning to write you and Phil a long letter – I didn't know if I should say anything –

Dolly (*over some of this*) She wants us *not* to talk about it.

Franny That's what I would have thought –

Dolly So it'll heal, she says.

Franny That's why I didn't –

Dolly Right, Sal?

Sally looks at them and nods.

Sally Whatever you think is best. I don't know.

She smiles at her younger cousins, then:

So – Grandma's looking good, I think. Don't you?

Franny We see her all the time, so – I'm glad you think so.

Dolly (*Laughing*) Father's finally got her off her little tractor.

Sally She wasn't still –?

Franny Just for the lawn.

Sally Still.

Dolly Yeah.

Sally I'm sure that wasn't easy.

Franny What?

Sally Getting Grandma off the tractor.

Franny No. It wasn't.

No one knows what to say.

Sally (*nods to the bedroom*) I'm sorry if it's a bit messy in there.

Franny No, it's –

Dolly No.

Sally The – cradle, we've been trying to – give away, but . . . (*Looks at herself.*) I'm the only one *not* getting dressed. I better . . . (*Moves towards her bedroom.*)

Franny I should go. I'm meeting – Betty in –

Sally (*suddenly*) Not yet! Stay another minute. I want to show you both something!

She has run off into her bedroom.

(*Off.*) It won't take long.

Dolly What's she . . .?

Franny shrugs.

Franny I have to go.

Dolly Any message you want passed along?

Franny ignores her.

Just thought I had to ask. She'll want to know.

Franny *If* she shows up, Dolly. Have you thought about that? If Mother *deigns* to turn up.

Sally returns with her guitar, tuning it.

Sally (*as she tunes*) I'm supposed to play for this – There's a class. He's a fantastic singing teacher. I think he'll take me. But I have to sing . . . (*Tunes, then to Dolly.*) I told you one of my friends auditioned for – the show you're seeing. *My Fair Lady.* And I've got a better voice than she does. (*Strums, to a worried Franny.*) If you have to go.

Franny No, I'm . . . I have time. How long do you –?

Sally You really want to hear it? Both of you? Really?

'Sure', 'Yeah', etc. from the girls

I didn't know what to choose, then I thought a kind of jazzy –

127

*Starts to strum chords and begins to play and sing a
slightly jazzy version of 'Hernando's Hideaway' from
Pajama Game.*

(*Sings.*) I know a dark secluded place
A place where no one knows your face
A glass of wine a fast embrace
It's called Hernando's Hideaway
Olé!

*Girls listen politely, without criticism. Sally smiles,
strums louder as she gets more and more into it, even
making castanet sounds on the face of her guitar with
her fingernails.*

(*Sings.*) All you see are silhouettes
And all you hear are castanets
And no one cares how late it gets
Not at Hernando's Hideaway.
At the Golden Finger Bowl or any place you . . .

*She stops, feeling self-conscious, even embarrassed.
During the song, Grandma appears in the doorway,
mostly dressed now.*

Grandma (*when Sally stops playing*) That's so good,
Sally.

Franny Terrific, Sal. Really. I'm sure that teacher's going
to love it.

Sally You're just saying –

Franny No. I mean it. I do. Ask Dolly. I have to go.

Dolly It was great.

Franny I'll see you tonight. I'll be back tonight.

And she hurries out.

Grandma Where is she meeting . . .?

Dolly Betty. I don't know. But she knows.

Sally has continued to pluck the guitar.

Sally (*to no one*) I love that song. It's so much fun.

Franny bursts back in.

Franny Sal, the phone's ringing out there.

We hear it in the hallway.

What should I . . . ?

Sally (*handing Grandma the guitar*) I'll get it.

She follows Franny out into the hallway, leaving the door open.

Dolly We have to go soon, Grandma.

Phone stops ringing. Sally has picked it up.

You should get dressed, come on.

Grandma I'm almost ready.

She hands Dolly the guitar and heads for the bedroom. Stops.

I only heard the end, but that sounded . . . good. Did it to you?

Dolly It did, Grandma.

Grandma It's nice to hear her sing.

She goes into the bedroom. Outside a siren goes by. Sally hurries back in and runs to the window and shouts.

Sally Franny! Franny!!

Grandma (*from the bedroom*) Is anything –?

Sally It's fine, Grandma. (*To Dolly.*) She heard me. I know Franny heard me. She just didn't want to hear me. It was your father.

Dolly Father? What's wrong? Is something –?

Sally suddenly sees her with the guitar.

Sally Don't touch that! Put that down! I just tuned it!

Dolly, stunned, puts the guitar down.

(*Suddenly guilty.*) I didn't mean it that way. I didn't mean you couldn't touch it. I'll teach you to play a few chords, if you want. It's just that when someone doesn't know how to . . .

Dolly Sure. I'm not going to touch it.

Sally I didn't mean –!! (*Stops herself. Trying to be calm, then turning back to Dolly.*) Do *you* know where she's meeting this guy? You know about the guy? Of course you do. Is he her boyfriend?

No response.

Grandma's going to have a fit. She's my responsibility. If you come and stay with me, I think it's only fair . . .

Dolly How did Father find out about the guy?

Sally looks at her.

Sally Your stepmother found a letter in Franny's bureau.

Dolly What was she doing in Franny's bureau?!

Sally (*over the end of this*) I don't think that makes any difference now!

Dolly She shouldn't be in our rooms!

Sally He read me part of this letter! How this guy has a friend with an off-campus apartment. How this friend is away this afternoon. How he's got the key, everything but the size of the bed! Your father's so upset. She doesn't know what she's doing. She's a kid.

Dolly I hate her. Not my sister.

Sally I don't know what to tell . . . (*Looks towards the bedroom.*) Your father's ready to get on a train.

Dolly He won't. He just says things like that. Maybe now they'll stay out of our rooms.

Sally She's only seventeen. When I was seventeen –

Dolly You going to tell Grandma?

Sally Won't your father tell her when you get home?

Dolly I don't think anyone tells Grandma too much any more. (*Short pause.*) My stepmother was looking for Franny's diaphragm.

Sally turns, confused, when she hears this.

Last week she accused Franny of owning one. Franny denied it, of course.

Sally suddenly laughs.

Sally Where would Franny get a dia—?

Dolly But she brought it with her. So that's why she didn't find it.

Grandma comes out, with a sweater.

Grandma Will I need a sweater? Is it going to be like yesterday?

Sally It's going to be warm, Grandma.

Grandma goes back into the bedroom to put back the sweater.

131

(*To Dolly.*) So this – 'guy'. It's nothing special. Something she does all the time. Since she's got the diaphragm . . .

Dolly shrugs.

I'm sick. Just don't tell Phil. He's a real prude when it comes to certain things. It's the Midwest in him. And he still thinks of you girls – as kids.

Grandma comes out, straightening herself.

Grandma You've got the tickets?

Dolly Yes, Grandma.

Grandma (*not listening, to Sally*) Phil gave us four tokens before he left for work this morning.

Sally He told me he was going to do that. You sure you don't want to take a – (*cab*)?

Grandma (*to Dolly*) What is so important about Gimbels? Look at the mess we've left. We shouldn't leave you with –

Sally There is no mess. Please. Go. And have a wonderful time. I hear it's a terrific show.

Grandma (*to Sally*) You think I look sophisticated enough for a Broadway show?

Dolly Good luck with the audition.

Sally What??

Grandma (*to Dolly*) I don't want to look like I come from the boondocks.

Dolly The singing audition. To get into that –

Sally Oh, right. Thanks! Bye!

Grandma (*to Dolly*) You'd tell me if I didn't look right. Your grandfather wouldn't, he'd let me –

Door is closed. They are gone. Silence. Street noise.
Sally does not know what to do with herself. She
fiddles with the guitar, starts to play, stops. She takes
the guitar into her bedroom. She returns and begins
picking up. Outside the window she hears children
playing. She goes into her bedroom and turns on the
radio. Music plays. She returns to get her cigarettes.
Hears the children and goes to the window to watch.
As she sits on the sofa, Older Franny (still of course
dressed as Grandma) enters and speaks to the audience.

Older Franny I hadn't heard Sally call after me; or if I
had it hadn't registered as anything more than one more
sound among the millions and millions of sounds which
make up Sullivan Street.

Sally lies back on the sofa and curls up.

At the corner I waded into Bleecker, as one wades into
any fast-moving river, cautiously, but with pleasure, and
hurried – if you can be said to hurry when you are
watching everything – toward the Riviera Cafe.

Sally has fallen asleep.

Our meeting spot. My boyfriend had sent me the address.
I expected to find him waiting, impatient, with a 'why-
are-you-always-late' look upon his face. The kind that I
could only wash away – with a kiss. But he wasn't there,
waiting for me. (*Beat.*) I took a table outside and ordered
coffee. I think it was the first time I ever ordered coffee
in a restaurant. I watched the people go by. The couples.
The attractive young men in their sleeveless summer
shirts. I felt like you feel on a beach with the waves
breaking across your ankles, legs, thighs, and then
running away. That's how the people outside the Riviera
came and went. Like waves. I could sit here all day, I
said to myself. (*Beat.*) There was a phone booth on the
corner and the first two times I tried my boyfriend his

line was busy. The third time he picked up. I've been waiting at the Riviera, I said. Did I get the time wrong? (*Short pause.*) You see, he said in a rather – happy voice, he'd met this girl, just the weekend before, and he really wished he could tell me in another way – I deserved that – and by the way, there's lots of fun things I could do in New York by myself, did I want a list? And hey, would I like to meet his new girl, she's real real nice, and the two of us would really really get along, and to this day I remember not so much what he said, but the smell in that phone booth, a mixture of stale cigarette smoke, some half-eaten thing that had sat in the sun too long, and urine. Anyway, I hung up on my boyfriend, and threw up in the booth. Now if a teenage girl throws up in a phone booth in the middle of Millbrook, half of the town would be there to find out what was wrong and to tell your parents. Suffice it to say that in New York or at least in Greenwich Village people are more respectful of your privacy. At least that's how I like to think of it.

I went back to my table and paid for my three coffees. I felt a little faint and found the bathroom – a tiny, dirty room with a hook to lock the door. I sat on the toilet seat, rubbed a wet towel across my face and tried to stop crying.

I think I did faint. But I guess didn't hurt myself when I fell. Someone shouted through the door to see if I was all right. I suppose they'd heard this thud or something or maybe just my sobbing.

I left the Riviera intent on spending the rest of my one day in New York walking and seeing first-hand what I'd imagined a million times. But instead, I found myself walking the few blocks back to Sullivan Street, staring for who-knows-how-long at the fire escape on the front of the building which for all the world now looked like an insect climbing up, then walking up the three echoey flights of cold stairs, until I was back here –

Door opens, Franny comes in, her clothes messy, her eyes red from crying. She stands in the doorway.

– where I'd convinced myself I'd first change my tear- and vomit-stained clothes, but where I also knew, in my heart of hearts, I'd never leave for the rest of the day.

Sally does not stir. She is asleep on the couch. At first Franny hadn't noticed her, but now she does.

I'd expected to find the apartment empty, which is why Sally'd given me my own key.

She sets the key on the table.

But it wasn't. Sally was still there, still in her nightclothes, curled up on the sofa, asleep.

Franny notices the music playing in the other room. She watches Sally for a moment.

What I didn't know then, and wouldn't know for years, was that Sally had had no intention of going out that day. Just as she'd had no intention of going out the day before or the day before that. Just as she'd no intention of ever leaving her apartment again.

She watches Sally.

And this is how she'd spent every day since the death of her baby. (*Beat.*) At the time, though, I knew none of this. At the time, I thought only about how much I hurt. And how much I needed a bed to cry on.

Franny goes into the bedroom, closing the door.

SCENE FOUR

Middle of the afternoon.

The radio is still on in the bedroom, though a different song is heard. The street noise has a different quality – slower, easier than in the morning. Hallway door opens, Phil enters carrying a couple bags of groceries – he does all the shopping, chores, etc., since Sally no longer leaves the apartment.

Sally is still asleep, curled up on the sofa. She stirs when he closes the door, but does not wake up.

Phil takes the bags to the kitchen table and begins to unpack.

Throughout the entire scene the music plays on the radio in the bedroom.

Sally (*waking up*) What's . . .? (*Sees Phil.*) What time is it?

Phil (*putting groceries away*) About four in the afternoon.

Sally Anyone . . . (*else here*)?

Phil shakes his head, then:

Phil I see you haven't even gotten dressed.

Short pause.

Sally (*smiling*) Come here. Come here. Sit with me.

He ignores her.

Phil (*unpacking*) I got some nice chops for tonight. He trimmed the fat off for me. I'm getting good at this. Look at these.

Holds one up. She looks at the chop.

(*Finally.*) Have you even washed? Your grandmother's here. Your cousins. What are you doing?!

Sally (*suddenly smiling, changing the subject*) You want to hear something about my little cousin –?

He turns away.

I was going to my audition!

Phil No you weren't.

Sally I was!! Don't you talk to me like that, you creep! (*Beat.*) I was going.

He unpacks. She smokes.

I don't sleep at night. I fell asleep. I must look a mess. (*She looks at him.*) You could say something. 'No, honey, you don't look a mess. You look sweet.' 'I love it when you just wake up.' 'I love that little girl look you have then, I –' I remember, Phil. Word for word. (*Looks at him.*) He's even stopped listening. (*Big sigh, then:*) What was I –? My little cousin, Franny.

You know what she's doing right now? Little Franny's out fucking some boyfriend. That's what all this was about. Her wanting to come down here. See a college? Lies. (*Explaining.*) The stepmother up there – what's her name? – found a letter. What the hell she was doing going through her stuff, I don't know, but . . .

Right now, in some crappy student apartment, she's fucking him. Maybe even next door. (*Pretends to listen*) Shh. (*Laughs.*)

The door to Franny's bedroom has slowly opened a little. Neither Phil nor Sally notices this.

Phil Let her fuck, so what? What's wrong with that?

Sally (*suddenly*) What's wrong with fucking? I don't know, Phil. You tell me.

Looks at him. She gets up and looks at him across the kitchen table. As she leans, she nearly exposes her breasts.

What is wrong with it?

She tries to touch him, but it is clear he can't even touch her.

What else besides the chops are we having for dinner?

Phil Mashed potatoes. String beans. I thought we'd go get Italian ices for dessert. The kids I thought would like that –

Sally What kids? Have you heard a word I said? I wouldn't call running off with – And she's got tits like – Bigger than mine. I suppose you like that. And she knows what she's got too. (*Beat.*) So do you think she's attractive?

Phil Sally, what are you talking about?

Sally Is she the type you'd fuck?

No response.

You've got to be fucking someone, and it certainly isn't me.

Phil Don't be pathetic.

Sally A little late for that.

He tries to ignore her.

I should get dressed. After all, we have guests. (*Beat.*) I was dreaming of our baby. That's the dream you woke me from. (*Trying to make a joke.*) You should apologise for that. (*Then:*) That's why I woke up smiling. She was all right, you'd be happy to know. She was maybe three. She was running. And smiling. She could talk. I loved her little voice. When Dolly was three I used to babysit her, so maybe that's why . . . The spark. (*Beat.*) Anna running through the park. Or maybe it was in the country. Grandma says Dad would help us get the house. Back home. I told her – I'm going to be an actress. I am an actress! I need to live here. I need all the city has to –

Phil So get out of the house.

This stops her, then she tries to stay calm.

Sally I will. (*Heads to the bedroom. Stops in the doorway.*) I'd expect you to be a little more – understanding. We all have our crutches . . . (*Beat.*) Look at you, Phil. Sometimes I think we need to look at you. You used to say going to church was for your parents and other hypocrites and phonies. Remember saying that?

Phil You've done this already, Sally.

Sally (*continuing*) That you didn't need that crap. Real *thinking* people saw through all –

Phil I went once! I shouldn't have told you.

Sally But you did. (*Forces a smile.*) And now who's the hypocrite, Phil? Who's the phoney just like your parents? Who got on his little knees and prayed: 'Oh dear God, help me! Help me! Take away these evil thoughts I have about doing harm to myself!'

Phil (*erupts*) I shouldn't have told you!!

Short pause.

Sally That – was a reaction. Thank you.

She goes into the bedroom. Phil takes out a beer and opens it. In the bedroom, Sally takes off her nightgown and puts on a skirt. She comes back out, straightening the skirt. She is naked from the waist up. She comes up to Phil, pretending to fix her skirt.

Phil Don't walk around like that in front of the window.

Sally Why? It's our home. (*Walks in front of the window.*) Actually, I seem to recall *you* saying something like that –

139

to me. (*Half to herself.*) 'Sal, it's our home. We can walk around any way we want.' (*To him.*) I think this was right after your suggesting I take off all my clothes. (*Teasing, trying to be seductive.*) 'You mean, I don't have to wear . . . ?' And you put your finger to my lips, and whispered: 'You're home. You don't have to wear anything.' (*Beat.*) 'You don't have to wear that.' And you touched me. 'Or that.' 'That.' (*Looks at him, smiling.*) Remember? And we didn't close the shades either. (*She goes up to him.*) And *I* said 'You don't have to wear –'

Phil Get dressed, Sally. You want your grandmother to come home and find you like this?

Sally You mean, like I am? Like we are?

He turns away. Sally approaches him from behind. She presses up against his back. She rubs her breasts against him, trying desperately to interest him. She reaches around to try and hold him. He is shaking his head. Gently he pushes her hands away. She reaches down and tries to touch his groin, he pushes her harder away. And she erupts. Suddenly she starts hitting him on the head and back, while at the same time trying to press her breasts against him, as if two contradictory impulses were happening to her – her anger and her need. Neither says anything or makes a sound. Sally just continues to hit – Phil makes little effort to protect himself – and press herself on him, touch him, get him to touch her: a grotesque moment of self-abasement. The door to Franny's bedroom suddenly closes. Phil and Sally stop when they hear the noise. Phil goes to the door and knocks. Nothing. As he reaches for the knob, the door opens – Franny is there.

(*Suddenly seeing Franny.*) What are you doing here?! (*Turns to Phil.*) Did you know she was –?

She covers her chest.

Phil No.

Franny I was – writing in my journal . . .

She holds up her journal that she has been clutching.

Sally How long have you been here?

Franny I just got in.

They stare at her.

I was writing. In my journal. I just started. Excuse me.

SCENE FIVE

In the dark, a voice (Grandma's) calls out.

Grandma Franny! Dinner!

Franny opens the bedroom door: Grandma, Sally, Phil and Dolly are finishing setting the small kitchen table for dinner. They are talking as they finish setting things out and taking their seats at the crowded table. Street noise from the window. Early evening.

(*To Sally.*) Your father's even picked out one house.

Sally Which one? Do I know it?

A glance at Phil.

Grandma On Chestnut. The white one with the gables?

Sally What happened to the couple who –?

Grandma He's retired. And the stairs are too much.

Sally (*to Phil*) Remember that house? I drove you by it –

Grandma (*at the same time*) And they have a son in Baltimore, so they're thinking –

141

Sally How did Father know it'd –?

Grandma Did you ever talk to him about it?

Sally (*to Phil*) I didn't. I swear. Anyway, we're staying here.

Franny has slowly moved to the table.

Franny Where am I supposed to –?

Sally Get a chair and push in. This isn't formal. (*Laughs to herself. To Franny.*) You didn't hear us setting the table?

Franny I –

Everyone is digging in, passing the food, commenting: 'Dig in.' 'Looks great.' 'These chops are so lean.' 'Phil had them cut off the fat. He's a good shopper.' etc. While Franny drags a chair to the table and sits, squeezing in. Out of this innocuous table conversation comes:

Sally Phil was saying when we were making dinner – Tell them. (*Reaches over and touches his hand.*)

Phil About?

Sally (*smiles to everyone*) Work today. Your guest.

Grandma What??

Phil An important writer came to the office today, it's a publishing office so how strange is that?

He laughs. No one else does.

Grandma Who was this writer?

Phil I don't think you'd –

Sally Tell them.

Phil Edmund Wilson. Do you know . . .? (*No one does.*)
He's . . . fat. (*Laughs.*) Mr Farrar and Mr Cudahy were
showing him around. We had to almost stand at attention.
The three of us in publicity. He won't give interviews.
He won't promote his books at all. He even showed us a
little card he hands out that says 'I won't give interviews.
I don't give autographs. I don't –' whatever. He seemed
to think that was clever. (*Beat.*) And I suppose maybe it
is – to anyone except the someone whose job it is to
promote his damn books. (*Takes a bite of food.*) He's a
good writer though. Worth the trouble. That's what I'm
told.

    *Pause. They eat. No one is interested in Phil's story,
    but he continues.*

He'd sold his new book to another publishing house –
Doubleday. So they were trying to woo him back. That's
what it was all about. I learned this . . . (*Short pause.*)
Anyone want to know any more about it?

    No response.

Grandma (*turns to Franny*) How was your tour of the
college?

Sally Yes, let's hear about that.

Grandma Did you like it?

Franny Sure.

Grandma You met up with your friend all right?

    Sally looks at Franny.

Franny I did.

Grandma She was helpful?

Franny She was.

Sally (*being mean*) Tell us what you liked most about the college.

Franny looks at the others, then:

Franny The library's neat. I liked that.

Sally You liked the library. Spend much time in the library with your friend?

Franny Enough. But she had a lot of studying to do, so that's why – as you both know – I came back early. (*Takes a bite.*) So how was *My Fair Lady*? I haven't heard a –

Grandma We've talked about that. Dolly will tell you later –

Sally Tell her now. She should know just what a little conniving sister –

Phil Stop it.

Sally (*to Franny*) Your sister planned, it appears, a little more than a trip to a show. They're in Gimbels, she and Grandma and . . .

Turns to Grandma, who says nothing.

They're looking at sweaters? It was sweaters, right?

Grandma Yes.

Sally And suddenly Dolly looks at her watch. 'Oh my God,' she says. 'Let's go to the perfume counter.' 'Why?' says Grandma. 'You want to look at sweaters, don't you?' But Dolly nearly drags Grandma to the perfume counter. The clock strikes twelve and guess who is waiting there?

Franny Mom.

Reaction from the others.

Sally She knew. She's a part of this. (*To Grandma.*) I told you this.

Franny (*over this, to Dolly*) Was she alone or did she –

Dolly Alone.

Sally She wouldn't have the guts to bring him. Isn't it enough to – And what's Grandma supposed to do?

Grandma She was made up like a –

Dolly She looked beautiful.

Franny I'm sure she did. How long were you with her at the perfume counter, Dolly?

Grandma A couple of minutes.

Franny Oh.

Sally Then they had lunch.

Franny (*amazed*) Together? I didn't know you were going to have –

Dolly Mom bought us lunch.

Franny (*to Grandma*) Yours too, Grandma?

Grandma shrugs as if to say 'What could I do?'
Franny starts laughing.

Sally What's funny?

Phil (*to join in*) Where'd you eat?

Dolly (*looking at Franny*) Some place called – Dempseys?

Sally (*over this, to Franny*) And she went to the show too. Little Miss Arranger had worked everything out.

This gets Franny laughing again.

She'd sent away –

Franny Who paid for – ?

Dolly Dad.

A burst of laughter from Franny.

But Mom's paying him back.

Sally He won't take money from her.

Dolly (*to her sister*) We had seats together. Mom sat next to me. She misses us so much, Franny.

Franny stops laughing.

Sally (*after a quick glance at Phil, to Franny and Dolly*) What that woman did to your father. You don't treat a husband like that.

Phil She fell in love.

Grandma I think it's best if we don't say a word about this to their father.

Short pause. Franny stands, taking her plate to the counter.

Phil You're done? You haven't eaten –

Franny I'm not hungry.

She looks to Dolly.

Sally (*eating*) Your first time in New York. And you arrange tickets, lunch, a meeting with – We're going to have to watch her, Franny. She's sneaky. (*To Phil.*) Think of the position she put Grandma in. What could she be thinking?

Phil (*eating*) That she wants to see her mother. That's all she's –

Sally That woman's a whore.

Dolly gets up and takes her plate to the counter, joining her sister.

(*To Grandma.*) And I'm serious, you're really going to have to keep an eye on Dolly. If this is how – Lying to us. Stealing –

Phil What did she – (*steal*)?

Sally Money for the theatre tickets, from her father.

Dolly (*to Sally*) Mom's paying that back.

Sally (*continuing*) Money for a trip that was supposed to be about – something else. I know we're not that much older than those two, Grandma, but that only means we (*Phil and her*) remember what it's like. At their age. So there are problems, but you have to control yourself. That's what growing up means, girls. (*Back to Grandma.*) Aren't I right? (*Grandma hesitates, then nods.*) This is for your benefit, girls, please. I'm not trying to be mean. (*To Phil.*) Am I?

Phil No.

Sally reaches over and touches Phil's hand. He eats.

(*To Grandma.*) I remember sitting with their (*Franny and Dolly's*) father – he took me into his study – After their mother had left. I felt sort of flattered that he chose me, though maybe he was talking to anyone. (*Laughs.*) But I was flattered. And all he talked about was how much he loved those two girls.

Grandma nods.

How they're his life. His two daughters.

Sally (*to Phil*) I don't think he talked to everyone. I think he chose you. Just like *my* father chooses to confide in you. (*To Grandma, explaining.*) When we visit? You raised two great sons, Grandma. How did you do it?

147

Grandma Luck, I suppose – (*Laughs to herself.*)

Sally What?! (*Looks to Phil, then back to Grandma.*)
Tell us what's funny.

Grandma Those two boys weren't always so good.

Sally (*a little too excited*) My father?! Oh!

*Laughs, then suddenly turns to Franny and Dolly at
the counter.*

Listen to this, girls. Grandma's going to tell us about our
fathers – when they were boys.

Franny and Dolly don't move.

Grandma They were – wild boys.

*Big whooping laugh and clap of the hands from Sally.
Smile from Phil.*

Now they're – the two most strait-laced men you'd find –
anywhere.

Franny and Dolly certainly agree with this.

But –

Sally Didn't they fight a lot as boys?

Clearly Sally has heard these stories before.

Grandma Fight? They were at each other's throats.

Laughter from Sally.

I remember –

Sally (*excited, to Phil*) Here comes a Grandma story.

She touches Phil's hand again.

Grandma (*to Phil and Sally, sincerely*) You are such a
wonderful couple. (*Quickly continuing.*) When Edward

won that red bicycle in the grocery store contest, Robert was beside himself.

Sally looks back to the girls on 'Robert'. Clearly Robert is the girls' father.

'Thou shalt not covet thy brother's bike.' Isn't that one of the Ten Commandments?

Laughter. Grandma obviously isn't that funny, but she's getting a great response from Sally. Lights begin to fade. Franny and Dolly remain at a distance, stone-faced.

Anyway – he 'borrowed' it. And there he is riding his brother's bike, coming down a gravel hill, and he tries to turn – I can still see Edward's face. I've never seen something *that* red . . .

The last image we see is that of Franny and Dolly watching from a distance.

SCENE SIX

Later that night.
Jazz music is heard coming from the window. It will play throughout the scene. The room is mostly dark, only a single light is on. Franny and Dolly are alone together. Dolly is holding a letter. Franny sips a beer.

Dolly She's so beautiful. I guess I forgot that. After two years you forget. When I was nearly at the perfume counter –

Franny Dragging Grandma.

Dolly (*smiles*) Yeah. And she came around –

Franny (*trying not to sound interested*) What was she wearing?

149

Dolly Dark-blue dress, with a white print. With straps, little cape. The dress went right below the knee. A funny wonderful little hat, she wore angled. Mom can wear things that other people . . . Gloves.

Franny White?

Beat. Dolly shakes her head.

Dark-blue?

Dolly nods.

Dolly You going to open it? (*The letter.*)

Franny ignores her.

She didn't seem –

Franny (*interrupting*) What?

Dolly I mean after what we'd been told – She seemed to – She started crying, Franny. *She* started . . .

Franny Mom cries easily.

Dolly Does she?

Beat.

Franny Yeah. It means nothing.

Dolly I thought Grandma was going to have a heart attack.

Franny smiles.

I think it took her half an hour before she realised that I'd . . . You know –

Franny That you hadn't just run into –

Dolly Yeah.

They both laugh, then silence.

Open it. It's to you.

Franny hesitates, then takes the letter and opens it. Finds a photo, looks, then has to close her eyes – the emotion is too great.

How old are you there?

Franny (*suddenly*) You know I don't believe a word she says. And you shouldn't either. She's only going to hurt you. If she had wanted to see us –

Dolly She said she's tried. She's had a lawyer try. She's even called Father and begged –

Franny I can't imagine Mother begging for anything. Certainly not for us.

She starts to put the picture and the unread letter back in the envelope.

This was a mistake, Dolly –

Dolly She asked why we didn't answer any of *her* letters.

Franny What letters?

Dolly She's written tons of letters – to both of us, she said.

Franny And you believe her?! Oh Dolly!

Short pause.

Dolly (*picking up the programme of* My Fair Lady) I can't even remember the show. As soon as the lights went down, I guess so Grandma couldn't see or do anything to stop us, Mom reached over and took my hand and held it in hers.

Hands Franny the programme. Franny looks through it.

Then she pulled it to her, and pressed it against her chest. Then she kissed it. I put my head against her shoulder. She stroked my head. She touched my cheek. I looked up at her. We cried through the whole play. (*Beat.*) At the intermission, Mom went outside to smoke a cigarette. Grandma tried to buy me some candy, but I just followed Mom. Grandma said something about how 'You haven't given up that awful habit, have you Jennifer?' The cigarettes.

Franny nods. She understands.

Grandma wanted me to go inside with her, but I wouldn't. Then Mom snapped open her purse – I remember the purse – with thin gold stripes and a gold band –

Franny I don't remember the purses. (*Tries to laugh.*)

Dolly And took out a photo. And said here, Dolly, this is 'my man'. (*Short pause.*) That's what she said, called him – 'my man'. Grandma made this awful sound and sort of ran away – for an instant, 'cause she was back in a second, but not before I had a chance to look . . . Back inside, she slipped it into my hand, and I hid it in my programme.

Franny, realising, shoves the programme back at her. Dolly opens it and takes out the photo of their mother's lover.

Here he is.

Franny I don't want to see –

Dolly Look, Franny.

Franny (*erupts*) I don't want to see – 'her man'! Get it away from me!

She pushes the photo away. The hallway door opens and Sally enters, having used the bathroom.

Sally I'm done. Thank God I sneaked in there before Franny, or – (*Smiles.*) But I learned my lesson there.

Franny ignores her. So she smiles to Dolly, as if it was Dolly she'd been speaking to.

Dolly (*to say something*) Think what I go through at home.

Sally You must have the patience of a saint.

Dolly Thank you. I think I do.

Sally moves towards her bedroom.

Franny (*to Sally*) Can I go down to that – (*jazz*)?

Sally No. The night's over for you, young lady. And for all of us as soon as Grandma and Phil get back from their walk. It's . . . (*Starts to look for the time, then:*) And besides, I'd have thought after your day you'd be very, very tired. (*Forces a smile. Then half to herself as she heads for the bedroom:*) When I was seventeen, I didn't even know what a diaphragm was!

Sally has gone into her bedroom.

Dolly She knows about – Father called –

Franny I heard.

Dolly (*over this*) They'd found a letter, about how you were going to meet –

Franny So what? Does Grandma know –?

Dolly I don't think she told her –

Franny I don't care what they think. They're idiots. They are complete phonies. (*Beat.*) And so is Mom.

Dolly That's not true.

Franny How did she know about my dia—? (*Seeing Dolly's guilty face.*) Forget it. (*To herself, mumbling.*) Father and his bitch.

Suddenly, hits the chair or sofa.

Shit!

Beat.

Dolly And Mom is not a phoney.

Franny Believe what you want.

Dolly And by the way – she did say that she'd seen me in the play.

Franny What??

Dolly The play I was in. She saw it.

Franny No she didn't. She didn't even know about you being in the –

Dolly I'd told her about it. I'd called her and –

Franny You called her? Mom? When? You didn't have her number –

Dolly I had gotten it out of Dad's desk. There's a – divorce file. You know Father, he's so – (*organised*). I knew it was there. And I found it and I called her and I told her because I thought she'd really really want to know that I got the part of the young girl in *Our Hearts Were Young and Gay*. I thought she'd really want to know about my costume. Because she always made our costumes with us for Halloween. So . . .

Franny just watches her sister, who is close to tears.

And she couldn't wait to see me in the play, she said. I didn't ask her, I didn't make her, it's just what she said. (*Beat.*) And then she wasn't there.

Franny (*smiles*) Yeah.

Dolly But she *did* come. And she asked me if I liked her flowers. I never got any flowers. Did I?

Franny I don't remember any. What do you mean, Mom was there?

Dolly Remember the little boy playing the steward on the ship? And how he came on stage all proud and was suppose to be saying 'All ashore who's going ashore!' but instead shouted 'All aboard who's going ashore.' And then cried? (*Beat.*) Mom said that was her favourite part. I hadn't said anything about it, she told me . . . Her favourite – except of course for me. (*Smiles. Short pause.*) How could she have known –?

Franny Father probably told –

Dolly They don't talk!

Franny You believe her?

Dolly nods.

That she was there?

Dolly In the back, so Father –

Franny So no one could see – (*Stops herself.*) You never got any flowers. They were probably never sent –

Dolly When we left today – and we were hugging. Again I thought Grandma was going to die, but . . . We're hugging and she says how much she loves me. And you. And then she said . . .

Franny waits and listens.

Her last words today were – She said: 'Don't trust your father.'

Pause. The jazz plays in the distance.

How was *your* afternoon?

Franny Great. We pretty much wore out my diaphragm.

Dolly Is that what happens? They wear out?

Sally enters in a robe, and goes to the couch to read a magazine. She turns on a lamp, then suddenly realises.

Sally Oh, I know what you two have been doing.

Franny What?

Sally You little snoops.

Dolly What are you talking about?

Sally You've had the lights out.

They look at her, confused.

So you can spy on . . . (*Nods towards the window.*)

Franny At what?

Sally Aren't they there? (*Looks out of the window.*) Across the street. One floor higher. They often 'forget' to close their shades. (*Looks at the girls. A statement.*) You haven't seen them. So what have you been looking at?

Dolly We haven't been looking at –

Franny (*same time*) What is she talking about?

Sally A couple. About Phil's and my age. They walk around – without – anything. Right past the window. One, then the other. Sometimes one'll run past, then he'll hurry behind her. Then you don't see them for a while. (*Looking.*) I figure off to the left – that's their bedroom. They have a bathroom, I think. And to get to that they must have to pass . . . (*Beat, looking out.*) That's the – study or whatever. They've got a TV. You see the blue light sometimes. I've seen him sit – there's a chair. When he sits you can see his arm. Sometimes I think she sits with him or – on him. All you see is his arm, and her, like – (*Gestures.*) You sort of imagine what they're doing. (*Beat.*) Maybe they're just watching TV. Maybe they're talking politics. (*Smiles.*) But that's not what it looks like – with the arms. Once his arm was like – (*back to us*) And hers – turned the other way (*facing us*), and it's – lower, so she's, and at a certain moment, they held hands . . . (*Beat.*) You two probably don't understand, but you will when –

Franny You're imagining that she's sucking him off.

Short pause.

Sally That's correct. (*Looks at Franny.*) Don't think you can shock me. You can shock your grandmother. You can shock your father, but I see right through you. I see who you are – *and* who you think you are. And there's a real big discrepancy, my dear.

Pause. Looks out of the window. Smiles to herself.

Sometimes I think they look at us. We often – forget to close the curtain. And we walk around – Philip and me, like . . . I don't know when I've last worn pyjamas or a nightgown. And Philip of course wears nothing. (*To Franny.*) I'm sorry if this –

Franny If this what?!

Sally I mean – you two are just kids.

Smiles. Notices the beer on the floor next to Franny.

Is that a beer you have? Did Philip give you that?

Franny I took it myself.

Sally nods, thinking.

Sally I remember when I was your age, sneaking my first drink –

Franny It's not my first –

Sally (*over this, to Dolly*) Swallowing it really fast I thought I was so neat. So grown-up. I wasn't going to listen to what anyone said, I felt I could do what I wanted. Then the room started spinning, and then there was my father holding my head over the toilet bowl as I barfed up my guts. (*Laughs.*) It's not easy growing up. I know. Believe me, Franny, I know all about it. I've been there.

There is nothing to say. Finally she looks towards the door.

How long are Grandma and Phil going to be out?

No response.

I think I'll read in our bedroom. (*Picks up her magazine.*) Goodnight, Dolly. (*Looks to Franny, but decides not to get too close.*) Goodnight, Fran. I mean – 'Franny'. That's so cute. (*Goes into her bedroom.*)

Franny What a cow.

Dolly She's okay. She's gone through a lot.

Franny picks up her beer and takes a sip.

Franny Want some?

Dolly nods. She takes a sip.

Want your own?

Dolly nods. Franny goes to the refrigerator, takes out another beer, opens it, hands it to Dolly and lights a cigarette, as:

I hate her guts.

Dolly (*picking up Franny's letter*) You going to read this?

Franny ignores her, then looks out of the window.

Franny Someone's turned on the lights over there.

Dolly You know she (*Sally*) told Grandma and me this incredible dream she had. This morning when you were in the bathroom. She told us about what she dreamed last night?

Franny nods and continues to watch out of the window, sipping her beer and smoking. Jazz plays off.

She dreamed she'd just moved into a new town. Her family had moved – She was a kid, and they had a dog which they brought with them? And as soon as they moved in the dog died. (*Beat.*) And her father – I think he says something like, 'Let's not take it to the vet, that's just a waste of money.' So she's given the job to bury the dog. But then a neighbour, a new neighbour, because they just moved in and didn't know anybody yet, says that if she buries it, it'll only smell up the place, so he says she should cremate it. 'What's cremate?' she asks.

Franny She didn't know what –?

Dolly In her dream. She's that young.

Franny nods.

'Burn it,' he tells her. So she pours gasoline over the dog and lights a match. (*Beat.*) And as the dog goes up in flame – it starts to howl and scream something awful. She even mimicked what it sounded like. (*Tries to demonstrate.*) I can't do it like she did.

Franny now turns to Dolly and is interested or fascinated.

So she runs inside and gets her dad's twenty-two, hurries out and chases around this dog that's on fire and shoots it. Well all the neighbours are out now and watching, and everyone is horrified at what this girl's done – set a dog on fire and then shot it. And she knows that as long as she lives in this new town, that's what people will think of her. That's how she'll for ever be known. (*Beat.*) That's it. That was her dream. Amazing? You know the essay I have to write this summer about 'a real interesting character'? Well . . . (*Gestures toward Sally.*) It's going to write itself.

Franny I think she's pathetic.

Dolly She lost her baby, Franny.

Franny (*shrugs, then*) So get over it.

> *The hallway door opens, and Grandma and Phil return from their walk. Grandma is very tired, and Phil holds her by the elbow. Franny and Dolly hide the drinks and cigarette.*

Phil Sit down. I'll get you a glass of water.

Franny What's – (*wrong with Grandma*)?

Grandma I'm fine.

Dolly Sit down, Grandma.

Franny Sit down.

Phil Your grandma's a little tired. It was a bit longer walk than she thought. And it's been a long day.

Grandma I'm just sleepy. Really. What time is it?

Phil Nearly eleven.

Grandma I never stay up this late. Where's –?

Franny She's gone to bed.

Phil Her light's still on –

Grandma Don't bother her. (*Yawns.*) I should just go to – (*Taking the glass of water.*) Thank you.

*She sips. Tries to catch her breath. Others watch this
and say nothing.*

(*Feeling she is being watched.*) I'm not used to stairs.

Sally (*off*) Grandma! Is that you?

Phil We're back!

Grandma I should go and say goodnight to that beautiful
wife of yours. (*Goes into the bedroom.*)

Phil (*to Dolly*) You should be getting to bed too,
shouldn't you?

Dolly I'm not tired.

Phil What's that? (*He has noticed the beer.*) Have you
been –?

Dolly Maybe I will go to bed. Goodnight. Night.
Goodnight, Franny. (*Kisses her.*) Phil.

As he bends to kiss her, she tickles him and runs away.

Phil (*to Franny*) What about you?

Franny shakes her head.

Never going to bed?

*Franny smiles and shrugs as Grandma comes out of
the bedroom.*

Grandma Remind me to buy her a nice nightgown for
Christmas. I'll use the bathroom if that's –

*But before she can head there, Dolly runs out of their
bedroom, carrying her nightgown and hurries into the
hallway to use the bathroom.*

Phil (*as Dolly runs off*) Let your Grandma –

Grandma Maybe I'll get ready for bed first. I'll say my
goodnights in a minute. (*Tries to smile and heads off.*)

Franny She looks exhausted.

Phil She was fine. Then all of a sudden about four or five blocks away, I thought she was going to fall down. We had to stop every few feet. That's why we're . . .

Franny Dolly put her through a lot today. (*Beat.*) I think she thought she'd never see my mother again. And of course she has to be polite. Even – or maybe especially – when she hates someone she has to be polite. That must be hard. (*Beat.*) Not that I would know.

Phil is picking up around the room.

Phil I don't think a fifteen-year-old should be drinking beers. (*Noticing the ashtray.*) And smoking cigarettes.

Beat.

Franny Who cares what you think?

He turns towards his bedroom.

Phil (*noticing*) She's turned off her light.

Franny Better go to bed then.

He continues to pick up. She listens to the jazz.

You want to take me to that club?

Phil No.

Franny I'm old enough.

Phil I know.

Franny Then why not? (*Takes her beer back from him. Sips.*)

Phil (*incredulous*) What are you doing?

Franny I didn't finish that. I want to go there.

He looks at her, sipping her beer, a flirty pout on her face, and he approaches her, and suddenly dives at her and tickles her. She tickles back. Dolly enters from the hallway, now in her nightgown, sees what is happening and runs to join in: 'Get him! Get him! Not me, him!' 'Stop! Stop!' Then, as Phil is pushed off the sofa on to the floor:

Phil I give up! I give up!

Sally (*off*) Phil? Philip?

Pause. They stop and listen.

Phil?

He gets up and goes into their bedroom. Muffled voices from the bedroom: 'What are you doing out there?' 'Nothing.' 'Aren't you coming to bed?' 'In a few minutes.'

Dolly (*to Franny*) Don't forget the letter.

Phil comes out of the bedroom, stopping at the doorway.

Phil (*to Sally in the bedroom*) Would you like the door closed?

We don't hear the answer, but Phil doesn't close the door. As he turns back to the girls:

(*To Dolly, pointing.*) You – to bed.

Dolly Night. What about –?

Franny I'm coming. Let Grandma use the bathroom first.

Phil Goodnight.

Dolly goes off to their bedroom. Pause. Jazz plays.

Franny So you don't wear anything to sleep in?

Phil What?

163

He looks at her. She smiles. Then she turns and looks out of the window.

Franny They just turned their lights off.

Phil What are you talking about?

She stares at him.

(*Finally.*) What hasn't my wife told you about?

Dolly comes back out.

Dolly Grandma's asleep. She hasn't used the bathroom. Should I wake –?

Phil Let her sleep.

Franny Is she still in her clothes –?

Dolly No, she changed.

Franny Good.

Dolly starts to go back, stops.

Dolly Franny, you can use the –

Franny Thanks. I know. Goodnight.

Dolly goes into the bedroom. Phil sips from Franny's beer.

Phil 'Franny'. I think that's really neat, by the way. I've been meaning to say that.

Franny What?

Phil Changing your name. Because of the Salinger story. I think it's an incredible story.

Franny Me too.

Phil Obviously or you wouldn't have –

Franny Do you think she's pregnant or having a nervous breakdown? In the story. (*Beat.*) Franny.

Phil I know. I – maybe it's both.

Franny That's good. I hadn't thought of that.

Phil That's – what a lot of people think now. Anyway, it's a neat thing to do. If only my name were Zachary, then I could –

Both – be called Zooey!

They laugh. Short pause. Phil looks towards his bedroom, then:

Phil You've read 'Zooey'?

Franny In the town library. The school library doesn't get *The New Yorker* –

Phil I wouldn't think –

Franny And Dad forgot to get it in Poughkeepsie, when he went . . .

Phil I have a copy. But it's the only one –

Franny No, no, I –

Phil And it sold out in like – (*Snaps his fingers.*)

Franny I heard. Though not in Poughkeepsie.

He smiles. An awkward pause.

Phil (*finally*) Lying in your bathtub, smoking cigarettes, talking to your mother, who's sitting there, smoking cigarettes. And she's a vaudevillian. To me – that's New York. That became New York. You try and think, so what is the difference between Ann Arbor and New York? I think of Zooey in the bathtub. I don't know why really. (*Smiles at her.*) It seems so – I don't know. Sometimes this place can seem so scary. New York.

Franny nods.

And sometimes it's like it just sort of wraps its arms around you. The sounds, people . . . (*Drifts off in thought, then:*) You think you'll come here to go to school?

Franny shrugs.

What does your boyfriend say?

Franny He's – begging me to come.

Phil I'm sure.

Another pause. The jazz plays. Franny plays with the letter.

(*Noticing the letter.*) What's –?

Franny From my mother. I haven't read it yet. (*Short pause.*) What do you think he's going to write next? Salinger.

Phil shrugs.

Could be a million things. There's so much we don't know about – the twins. Waker? In the conscientious objectors' camp? What's that about? I think what Salinger's got to do is start putting things together. Show how the Glass family fits together. Right now it's just – bits, fragments –

Phil Fantastic bits –

Franny True. But I think he's only begun something . . . Something that is going to define our time.

Phil Huh.

Franny I can't wait.

Phil Me too. (*Beat.*) I'm going to bed when I finish this.

Franny Don't drink too fast.

Phil I won't.

Franny Sip and you'll remain standing. Father's advice.

Phil sighs, wipes the sweat off his forehead.

Earlier this summer I was in a show at home. I was a flapper. In the chorus. In my high-school gym. Something to keep the kids out of trouble. (*Smiles.*) God, was it hot in that gym. My dress stuck to my backside. (*Looks down at her backside.*) Kept having to pull it off. In the middle of a dance. (*Not thinking about what she is saying.*) I don't know if I want to be in theatre or not. Dolly wants to, but . . . I like books. I think I'm pretty enough though.

Phil You are.

Franny How's Sally doing with her acting? She doesn't seem to be doing much work right . . . now . . . (*Realises this is the wrong thing to bring up.*) I should go to bed. Goodnight.

She stands. Looks at Phil, then leans over and kisses him on the cheek. As she does, he turns to her. And they kiss on the mouth. She sits next to him, and they look at each other. She touches his face. He looks her over. He suddenly gets up and closes his bedroom door and turns off the lamp. He comes up behind her, touches her on the shoulder. She looks up at him, and as she watches him she reaches under her skirt and takes off her underwear. She puts her head against his hand. He kisses the top of her head. She suddenly turns and they kiss passionately. She rubs her hand across his chest and unhooks his belt. Still kissing, she unzips his fly. Her hand is in his crotch, his hands are up her skirt, under her blouse. Then at the height of this heavy petting Phil suddenly breaks away.

Phil No. I can't. Franny, this isn't right. This is wrong.

*He tries to get a hold of himself, breathes deeply. She
watches him. He zips up his trousers, hands her her
underpants. She watches. He then takes her hand and
squeezes it, and goes into his bedroom, closing the
door. Franny cries. She tries to get a hold of herself.
She turns on the lamp, notices the letter from her
mother. This makes her sob. She hides the letter under
magazines and continues to cry.*

Lights fade. Music fades.

*Immediately lights come up and new, wilder jazz
music plays from the club on Bleecker. It is two hours
later.*

*Franny is still on the sofa. She is awake and
listening. She is crying, and can't sit still, can't settle.*

*From Phil and Sally's bedroom: the sounds of the
couple making love. As they approach climax, the
noises/sounds/cries become more and more violent,
animal-like, and profound, as if something deep,
painful, uncontrollable is being touched and released.
Franny listens, then stands, goes into her bedroom
and closes the door.*

SCENE SEVEN

*The next morning. Street noise is heard out of the window.
Dolly is packing in the bedroom.*

*In Phil and Sally's bedroom doorway: Sally is finishing
up 'Hernando's Hideaway' on the guitar for Phil and
Grandma. Grandma is at the sink cleaning up. Phil is
getting dressed. Sally is still in a robe.*

Sally (*singing*)
At the Golden Finger Bowl or any place you go,
You'll meet your Uncle Max and everyone you know.

But when you go to the spot that I am thinking of
You will be free
To gaze at me
And talk of love!

*Franny enters from the hallway and goes into her
bedroom to finish packing.*

(*Singing.*) Just knock three times and whisper low
That you and I were sent by Joe –

Dolly enters with her suitcase.

Sally (*singing*)
Then strike a match and you will know
You're in Hernando's Hideaway
Olé!

Appreciative reaction from Phil and Grandma.

He's a fantastic teacher. I think he'll take me.

Grandma Of course he will . . . (*etc.*)

Sally (*to Phil*) What do you think?

Phil I think you're good. I always have. He'd be a fool
not to take you.

Grandma I can't believe she hasn't played that for you,
Phil.

Franny comes out with her suitcase.

Sally I didn't think he wanted to hear it.

Grandma Of course he did. Phil loves to hear you sing.
Did you hear what he said? What time is it?

Sally Oh God, the time!

Phil We're fine. There's –

Sally What time's their train?

Grandma I better strip the bed.

Grandma heads for her bedroom.

Sally You don't have to do that. Phil?

Phil (*following Grandma*) I'll do that, Marjorie.

Phil sees Franny.

Franny We're packed.

Grandma (*as she enters the other bedroom*) I love Sally's singing, don't you, Phil?

She goes into the other bedroom to strip the bed.

Sally (*to the girls*) Everyone slept so late. We slept so late. (*Smiles to herself.*) There's no time for breakfast. I'm sorry –

Franny Oh, we're not hungry. Are we, Dolly?

Dolly is hungry, but says nothing.

She's fine.

Sally There's some bread from last night –

Dolly I don't want to miss the train. Dad's meeting the train.

Sally (*smiles at them, then*) I wish you could stay longer. I really do. It's been really good having you here. (*To Franny.*) And next time – we'll have that boyfriend of yours over for dinner too.

Phil brings out Grandma's suitcases.

Phil was saying how he'd like to meet him.

Phil hurries back into the bedroom.

Grandma should tell you two about the house she went to see last night with Phil. He was telling me about it.

Franny What house?

Sally It's just a few blocks away. Where she lived.

Franny Where who lived?

Sally Our grandma.

Phil (*off*) Sal, Marjorie's making the bed!

Sally (*heading for the bedroom*) Grandma, I told you I'd make it!

Dolly In Greenwich Village? Grandma lived in Greenwich Village?

Franny When was this?

Sally has disappeared into the bedroom. Voices are heard off.

Dolly I don't understand.

Franny Me too. I don't understand anything.

Sally suddenly appears in the bedroom doorway.

Sally (*back to Grandma*) You think I should? Phil? Maybe I will. Maybe I'll come. (*Heads for her bedroom.*) Is there time? I have to get dressed.

Grandma (*coming out of the bedroom, to the girls*) Sally's coming with us to the train station.

Phil (*to Grandma*) She's coming with us. She's getting dressed.

Franny When did you live in Greenwich Village, Grandma?

Grandma A million years ago.

Franny You lived in New York City??

Grandma I must have told you that. I don't want to be one of those old ladies who is always repeating themselves.

Phil They don't know. Tell them. They're interested.

Sally (*coming out of the bedroom, getting dressed*) There's probably a lot you don't know about your grandma. Did you go inside? I meant to ask you that.

Phil I wanted to ring the bell.

Grandma (*to the girls*) I remember leaning out the second-floor window of that house and watching the soldiers march down Fifth Avenue, on their way to war.

Franny What war?

Grandma Us girls waving our scarves. (*Winks at the confused Dolly.*) Accidentally letting one go. Float down past the boys, to see if they would look up. And they did. (*Laughs.*)

Sally, listening, laughs, maybe a little too hard, from the other room. She is keyed up.

People were screaming. My husband, your grandfather was one of them. He says he probably marched right past me. But I never picked him out. There were so many boys.

Dolly How long did you live in New York City, Grandma?

Grandma A whole year. Maybe a little more. While Grandpa was at war.

Phil (*to Franny*) The First World War.

Grandma It's all changed now. It's all different.

Short pause. Everyone is a little confused, then, explaining:

The house. Where I used to live. I told you why I was sent to the city?

Phil You told me, Marjorie.

Grandma It's incredible now that you think about it.

Sally (*off*) I haven't heard this.

Grandma (*continuing*) But at the start of the war, your great grandfather had to hire all these day workers for the farm. All these – men. There was a lot of pressure to grow things for the war effort. So he needed a lot of men? Whatever kind of men he could get. (*Smiles.*) But he worried that maybe it wouldn't be right for me . . . So he sent me here! Sent me to New York.

The girls look at her, incredulous.

Franny He sent you to New York City to be safe from men?!

Grandma nods.

Incredible.

They burst out laughing.

Grandma (*over the laughter*) And it took my father a whole year to figure out what he'd done! And did I have fun!

More laughter. Then Sally, now dressed to go out, comes out. Phil and Grandma are nearly overcome with emotion.

Sally I'm ready, we should go.

Grandma You have everything? We haven't forgotten anything?

Franny I don't know.

Grandma Let me just check . . . (*Heads back into the bedroom.*)

Sally (*following her*) If you did, we can always mail it –

Phil is handing a magazine to Franny.

Franny What's this?

Dolly What is it?

Phil An old copy of *The New Yorker*. With a wonderful story in it.

Franny I can't take this. It's your only copy –

Dolly Let me see –

Franny No, you'll rip it.

She takes it.

Sally (*coming back out with Grandma*) What's that?

Phil Nothing.

Franny The Salinger story –

Dolly (*to Phil*) Why are you giving *her* presents?

Franny Because he likes me better!

Dolly He does, does he?

Dolly grabs Phil and tickles him, he fights back, tickling.

Sally (*to anyone who will listen*) I can't believe I'm taking you to the train!

Grandma Come on, girls. We're going to be late. Leave Phil alone. Come. Pick up your bags.

Sally suddenly joins in the tickling.

We have to go. Phil, why don't you walk with your wife?

They continue to tickle as she pushes them out.

Let's go. Girls, let's go. Girls!

They go out into the hallway, still trying to tickle each other. Grandma stays behind and again becomes the Older Franny. She speaks to us.

Older Franny And so I went home that summer. And tried to finish my Victorian Yorkshire novel – with no success. And tried to forget a boy – with a good bit more success. And tried to find a much better hiding place for my diaphragm.

Nine months later, my cousin Sally and Phil had a new baby. They came up to show her off, Uncle Edward took them to see the house on Chestnut, and they never left.

I did read Mom's letter – a few billion times. Dolly, my clever little sister, organised an unescorted 'shopping trip' that Christmas to New York City. We were to meet Mother in front of Saks. She appeared down Fifth Avenue, through a light snow, amidst the haze of the street lamps, her fur collar framing – that beautiful face. Like a vision – that is how she appeared to me; and that is just about how real, sadly, she proved to be. Dolly disagrees, and says I just should have spent time with her – like she did. (*Shrugs.*) Grandma lived only another five years. Women, it has recently dawned on me, die young in my family.

And little Annie? The baby? She's buried in Queens. For a while there was talk of moving her to Millbrook. But that stopped years ago. I think she's been forgotten.

Short pause. Street noise continues from outside the window.

As we get old, we start to see the – (*searches for the word, then*) fragility of – well everything. (*Short pause.*) But when we're young, thank God – we are oblivious.

Suddenly Franny charges back into the room. From down the hall cries of 'Franny!' 'We're going to miss the train!' 'We can send it to you!' etc.

Franny (*shouting back*) I'll just be a second!

She looks around, then hurries to the sofa, desperately searching for something she's forgotten. The Older Franny watches. Young Franny flips over magazines and finds what she is looking for – her mother's letter. She sighs, folds it. Then she suddenly notices something else, sticking out between the cushions in the couch: her underwear from the night before. She grabs them, looks around, doesn't know what to do. She tries to hide them on her body, then slides them inside the pages of The New Yorker *she is carrying, smoothing down the pages, as she hurries out*

(*Shouting.*) I'm coming!!

Older Franny looks out of the window as the street sounds continue: they are alive, music in the distance from Washington Square, cars, laughter, church bells, siren, and so forth.

End of play.

MADAME MELVILLE

One can take all possible liberties of line, form,
proportions, colours to make feeling intelligible
and clearly visible.

Pierre Bonnard

Madame Melville was first performed at the Vaudeville Theatre, London, on 18 October 2000, produced by Ostar Enterprises, Gregory Mosher, Freddy DeMann, Andrew Fell, and Adam Kenwright. The cast included:

Carl Macaulay Culkin
Claudie Irene Jacob
Ruth Madeleine Potter

Director Richard Nelson
Set Designer Thomas Lynch
Costume Designer Fotini Dimou
Lighting Designer Peter Mumford
Sound Designer Scott Myers
Associate Director Colin Chambers
Movement Jane Gibson
Voice Work Andrew Wade

Characters

Carl
Claudie
Ruth
Father

For Michael Nelson

*An apartment. Paris. 1966. Exit to the hallway and
front door, another to kitchen, a third to bathroom and
bedroom. Bookcases, record player and record albums, etc.*

*Carl, a fifteen-year-old American, reads to the audience
from a small paperback:*

Carl
                    'because she hath
A lovely boy, stolen from an Indian king . . .
But she perforce withholds the loved boy,
Crowns him with flowers and makes him all her joy.'

(He closes the book, and puts it back in the bookcase.)
I think I was nearly thirty before I saw an actual stage
production of *A Midsummer Night's Dream*. *(The book
is replaced, he turns back to the audience.)* The young
man speaking to you is the same age I was in 1966.
When I last visited this room. Which long ago ceased to
exist. Today I am nearing fifty myself, with wife and
children – one nearly fifteen himself – but I could not
find it in my imagination to see myself, to place the man
I am today here. In this room. For when I think of her,
or when I speak of her, in the middle of a thought, in the
middle of a dream, I am forever – a boy of fifteen. With
a voice like this boy's – honest, simple, thoughtful, and
not yet – uncertain. The uncertainty – that happened
here. *(He looks over the room one more time, then:)*
Recently I came across an interesting discussion of that
word by a professor in New Jersey. 'Uncertainty', he
said, 'is the tentativeness created from seeing many
things from many points of view.'

183

Short pause.

Uncertainty then is one of the first essential steps toward becoming a writer.

Beat.

The simple facts first. (*He smiles at the irony of this.*) What a devious, insidious phrase. (*Then, continuing.*) Anyway – we arrived in Paris in the winter, 1966.

Beat.

1966. When you felt the world about to burst its seams. They hadn't snapped yet, but you couldn't help but feel – any time.

Beat.

1966. My father, a businessman, had already been here six months, and when his project expanded we were brought over as well – my mother and me. My brother was at Cornell, smoking pot, he later confessed. And I was enrolled in the American School where I was taught literature by Mme Melville. I wasn't a very good student and hated Paris which seemed – with its streets, its monuments and its people – all created to make me feel stupid. I had few friends and with those I tagged along on Fridays to the Bus Palladium where – and this was supposed to excite me – we could dance like in America.

Beat.

It was at the Bus Palladium that I first heard the name the Rolling Stones – and where I first watched a young bearded American enthral a crowd of French girls as he burned what I learned through a series of breathless whispers was his draft card. Though when I saw this same young man burn it again another night, one had to wonder.

Beat.

Then, one day, out of the blue, Mme Melville, who had
hardly seemed to notice me in her class, asked – if I'd
care to join her and the small group of students who
met twice a week to see and discuss the very latest films.
(*He closes his eyes and recites.*) *Masculine Feminine.*
*Jules and Jim. Hiroshima mon Amour. Blowup. King of
Hearts.* (*Opens his eyes.*) It's where I saw my first naked
women – my first *moving* naked women – in these films.

Beat.

We'd all meet at her apartment. (*Gestures 'here'.*) I'd
return there as well for chocolates or cocoa or tea. She'd
always put music on.

*He moves the record player arm and a piece by Bach
begins to play.*

Music I was careful not to admit not knowing. Music so
beautiful . . . Music I had to ask, I had to wonder, why
did I not know such music? There was never any music
in my house – only what my brother played on his
record player. So I knew only that. I had never in my life
been to a concert – of such music. The other students in
the film group talked about how they liked so-and-so's
version of this-or-that better than someone else's version,
and I tried to agree. Tried to smile knowingly, but not
too aggressively as I did not wish to be actually brought
into the conversation. (*Turns and looks.*) And there were
books – books upon books, bookcases filled with books.
Both here and in her bedroom. In Mme Melville's
bedroom. (*Gestures.*) Through there.

Beat.

I looked at all these books, and while others around me
discussed what was in them – they had read them! – I –
I touched them.

Short pause. The Bach continues to play.

And so it was on one Friday evening, in early summer, with school nearly over for the year, that we watched a film about American surfboarders travelling the world looking for big waves, and we strolled as a pack back through the ghost-lit Paris streets, past the gates of the Sorbonne, and up the wiry toy elevator until we were here, where I, while in the toilet, heard first the doorbell, then voices, and the group's loud and many goodbyes.

From the hallway door, we hear these 'goodbyes' off.

And found myself suddenly in the middle of her living room, alone. So I picked up my jacket to go . . .

Claudie Melville, French, thirties, and very attractive, enters from the hallway. Carl pretends to be finishing zipping up his fly. Classical music plays.

Claudie (*surprised*) You're still here, Carl? You're not leaving with – ?

Carl (*over this*) Where are the others? I was – (*Gestures towards the toilet.*)

Claudie That was Sophie's mother. She was early. Were you getting a ride with – ?

Carl They live on the other side –

Claudie (*over some of this*) That's right. You're the one who takes the Metro. You live in the other direction. Whereabouts do you – ?

Carl Sixteenth –

Throughout this Claudie has appeared very distracted.

Claudie (*not listening*) Have some chocolates. No one ate any chocolates.

Carl I did.

Claudie Then have some more.

She takes a chocolate. Picks up a pile of mail, looks through it, sighs.
Carl watches her for a moment, then:

Carl I should go.

She turns and looks at him.

Claudie Sophie's mother came too early.

Carl (*explaining*) The Metro closes in –

Claudie Not yet. You've got a little bit of time. (*Continues to look through her mail, then looks up.*) Unless there's someplace you have to . . .

Carl No.

Claudie (*finishing with her mail*) Or I can drive you home. (*She sets the mail down, looks at him and smiles.*) And take off that tie. I detest ties on boys. And push back your hair. Straight back.

He does.

That's better. (*She goes to him and holds his hair back.*) I'm going to have a wine. What about you? Coca-Cola? Orangina? Mineral water? (*She heads for the kitchen.*)

Carl I'll have wine too.

She turns back to look at him, he pretends to look at her books.

Claudie If there's anything that interests you . . .

He looks up confused.

Take what you want.

Still confused.

Borrow a book.

He understands. She goes to the albums and pulls out one and hands it to Carl as she heads for the kitchen:

Claudie Put that on, will you please, Carl?

She goes, the music continues.

(*from the kitchen*) Did you see Lucy's skirt? Did you notice that? Of course you noticed that. You're a boy! The school rule says across the top of the knee. She must have rolled it up during the film. Is that what she did? You were sitting next to her.

Carl (*calls to the kitchen*) No. No, I wasn't. That was Robert.

Claudie (*entering with a glass of wine and a glass of Orangina*) Robert? Then perhaps *he* rolled it up.

Carl I don't think –

Claudie Here (*the Orangina*). I thought William was Lucy's boyfriend. That's not what I was feeling tonight. What happened to the – (*record*)

Carl I'm sorry . . .

As he puts on the new album:

Claudie Skirts are going way way up. That's what everyone's saying. Inches. Out of sight! As you Americans say. (*She smiles at him.*) Soon, you men will say – why bother. Right?

Before he can respond, the music comes, on: Stéphane Grappelli.

Shh. (*She sits on the sofa, kicks off her shoes, closes her eyes.*)

Long pause.
Claudie is lost in thought, as she sips her wine and gently sways to the jazz.

Carl watches her closely, then after a while takes out a new, unopened packet of cigarettes. He hesitates, then:

Carl Cigarette?

She opens her eyes and looks at him.

Claudie (*with a half-smile*) I didn't know you –

Carl I do. (*He doesn't.*)

She hesitates, then leans over him, puts her hand on his thigh for balance and takes a cigarette. She lets him light it. The music continues. She looks at his face, then brushes back his hair again.

It doesn't stay.

Claudie It will. We need to train it, so that after a while it won't dare not to. (*Smiles, smokes.*) What did you think of the film tonight?

Carl Not very much.

Claudie Because it was American?

Carl Why would that matter?

She shrugs.

I just got bored. A film about guys surfing . . .

Claudie It's very popular with the kids.

Carl I'm not a kid.

Claudie No.

Beat.

I liked seeing the boys in their bathing suits. That kept me interested. It kept the girls interested. Sophie says she's going to go back and see it again. And bring her mother. (*Laughs lightly.*)

Carl (*still serious*) I liked the films we've been seeing. The more serious ones.

Claudie This was serious.

Carl A bunch of rather thick guys going surfing.

Claudie About a bunch of 'guys' searching, Carl. On a quest – for that one perfect wave. It was mythological. Homeric. But not for you. Fair enough. You liked the French films about sex.

Carl They're not about –

Claudie How well are you doing in your other classes, Carl? I haven't heard about any problems, still –

Carl I'm fine.

Claudie You're a bright boy.

Carl Thank you.

Claudie You could do better in my class.

Beat.

You could speak more.

Carl I pay attention.

Claudie That's not what I said – I said you could assert yourself more. We'd all like to know what you're thinking. (*Changing the subject.*) I think Lucy's getting set to dump William. And I think it was for Robert that she was raising her skirt. What do you think?

Carl (*after a beat*) I think it doesn't have to be *for* anyone. That's not how everything always is.

Claudie I think you're wrong there. I think I'm right.

They listen to the music.
She sips, takes a puff, then as if suddenly realising:

Did you stay in the toilet until the others had left? Is that what you were doing?

Carl I didn't hear –

Claudie You didn't hear the bell? You didn't hear Sophie's very loud mother?

Carl (*over this, too emphatic*) No. No!

Claudie You didn't know everyone was leaving?

Carl No! (*He stands.*) I should go.

Claudie You weren't trying – on purpose – to stay behind? I think you were, Carl. And – I think there is nothing remotely wrong with that. (*He is frozen in place.*) But then again maybe you didn't know why you were staying back. I think men often don't know what makes them do the things they do. I think that is why women find men so – dangerous.

Beat.

And so – terrible. (*She is lost in her thoughts for an instant, then:*) And of course men find women dangerous for totally different reasons. Isn't that true? (*Smiles, sort of teasing, sort of flirting.*) We were talking about just this in class this week, weren't we? Drink your Orangina. (*He takes the glass and drinks, she continues without a beat.*) The books women have written about men – such as they are, and those by men about women. How different they are. It wasn't exactly on the curriculum, I snuck it in. Very bold of me, wasn't it? I looked to you two or three times in the discussion to join us. To tell us what you know about what men think about women. You must know a lot.

Beat.

Don't you?

He sits back down and drinks his Orangina. As she continues, he fiddles with the magazines etc. on the coffee table.

Next time – participate. Still I'm so happy you're in my class. So nice to see your attentive face there. Though I keep wanting to push that hair back.

She smiles. He looks up and half smiles. He has his hand on a magazine.

Look at that. Have you seen it?

Carl (*looking at the magazine*) No.

Claudie High school kids published that. From Pavini High School – do you know where – ?

Carl No.

Claudie *La Zanzara.* Do you know what it means?

Carl The mosquito.

Claudie Very good. Nice name for a student –

Carl I don't think so.

Claudie You haven't read – It's been in the news. Been all sorts of arguments – They discuss divorce, birth control, sexual education. High school students. Like you. The world is changing fast. If you wish to borrow that . . .

Carl I don't.

Short pause. He puts the magazine down, picks up a book.

Claudie That's right. It's not exactly your kind of thing, is it?

Carl What do you mean?

Claudie I mean – you wish to be a writer yourself, don't you?

Beat.

A poet, isn't it?

No response.

(*As if responding to his question.*) Who told me? Did Lucy tell me? (*She smiles.*) I think it was your father who told me.

Carl I didn't know you'd ever met my father.

Claudie Before you enrolled. He came to school to discuss you before he'd enroll you. We had a nice talk.

Carl He's never said he'd met you.

Claudie Why would he? Do you talk about me at home?

Beat.

And he might not even remember me. He saw so many teachers that day. But I remember very well him saying his son wanted to be a poet. And then he laughed. I didn't like your father.

Beat.

I said to him that the world needed all the poets it can get. How come you haven't shown me any of your poems? What are they about?

Beat.

Lucy?

Beat.

You *were* sitting next to her, Carl. You were sitting on her left. And I watched you manoeuvre to make sure you did too.

Carl Like I 'manoeuvred' to stay behind here?

Pause.

Claudie I'll tell you a funny story I heard on the radio. Hand me another of those (*cigarettes*). And look through (*record albums*) – if there's something you want to . . . (*hear*)

> *She lights her cigarette and puts her feet up on Carl's chair, against his leg.*

This man's a novelist. He's written maybe three or four published novels. One day he's riding the Metro and he sees the man next to him reading one of his books. He checks out what page he's on. Eighty-three. Well, he knows for sure there is a very funny incident on page eighty-nine. So he waits. He goes past his stop and waits. Then while the man is on page eighty-nine – the author watches him laugh out loud.

> *Beat.*

Then and there the writer decided to give up novels and write plays. (*Laughs.*) He needed an audience! So don't be a poet, Carl – be a playwright! (*Finishes her wine.*) I think we all need audiences, don't you? I was thinking getting our drinks – by the way there's more Orangina if –

Carl I drink wine.

> *Beat.*
> *She gets up and heads for the kitchen.*

Claudie I was thinking when I was in the kitchen, how nice – (*She is off and continues, off.*) – it is that you did stay back tonight. I really didn't feel like sitting here alone. (*She returns with a bottle of wine and a glass for Carl. For a moment as she sits she is lost in her thoughts, then:*) Sophie's mother came about a half an hour early.

Do you know Sophie very well? The conferences I have had about Sophie – I shouldn't be telling you this. (*She pours the wine.*) She's a real bitch. Not like your Lucy. Cheers. Or what do you say in America?

Carl I don't know.

She sits back down on the sofa and draws her feet up under her. Carl takes his wine. She sips hers, looks around, somewhat distracted, then noticing the magazine again:

Claudie So that high school magazine doesn't interest you.

Pause. The music is over. There is a silence in the room. Claudie doesn't know what to say, then:

Be a playwright! (*Toasts him, then finally:*) Now you say something.

Carl (*after a beat*) I did stay back on purpose. I waited in the toilet until I heard they were gone.

Puffs her cigarette, then:

Claudie Don't be too honest, it's not attractive.

He turns away, hurt.

But on the other hand, don't always just accept what a woman says. She's not always saying everything she means and that, I think it's fair to say, is an understatement. So – one can, a man can laugh at what she says. Put her in her place. No woman wants to be boss all of the time.

Beat.

It's your conversation now. Lead away. (*She waits, watches him, then:*)

Carl Are you a Catholic?

Claudie (*not what she expected*) Why do you – ?

Carl The cross (*around her neck*). And I saw on the toilet wall –

Claudie Yes, I'm a Catholic.

Carl Do you go to Mass?

Claudie I have.

Carl Could I go with you sometime?

Claudie You want to become a Catholic?

Carl I want to go to a Mass.

Beat.

There's a writer I like. A poet. I've been reading about him. He became a Catholic. So I'm interested in –

Claudie Not all good poets become Catholics.

Carl I know –

Claudie Not all poets who become Catholic are good –

Carl I know that, Mme Melville!

It is the first time he has used her name this evening. And the formality stops the conversation and changes its tone.

Claudie (*quietly*) You don't go to any church?

Carl My parents do. I don't.

Claudie Does that trouble them?

No response.

Anything else? It is still your conversation.

Beat.

And yes, I will take you to Mass if you wish. But let me

give you a little advice. When you are alone with a girl, don't, right off, start talking about religion. (*She smiles.*)

Carl Am I with a girl now?

She stops smiling.

Claudie No. No, you're not. (*Claudie leans over and looks through the albums. Without looking at him.*) Did you like the Grappelli?

No response.

We've just been listening to Stéphane Grappelli.

Carl I don't know what I like yet.

She continues to look.

How could I? And yes, I would very much like to borrow some books. That's why, to tell the truth – I stayed behind tonight. To see if I could –

Claudie (*without looking at him*) Please. Look.

Carl And the reason I hardly speak in school or here – or at the films – is because I don't have anything that's worth saying.

Claudie I doubt if you believe that.

Carl It's true. If you could hear some of my thoughts. Some of the things I've almost said? (*He tries to laugh.*) I laugh at myself all the time. Better me than you.

Claudie I wouldn't laugh –

Carl I'll tell you something that's true. At the beginning of the term, when the class books were handed out? I lined them up in my room at home. And measured with my hands their thickness and told myself – Carl, in a few more months you'll know at least this much. (*Shows the width with his fingers.*)

Claudie I'm not laughing. But speaking to you as a teacher now –

Carl How else have you been speaking?

Claudie (*over the end of this*) I would ask you, when you hear a new piece of music or see for the first time a great painting – not to worry how many 'inches' of knowledge is that? I'm saying, Carl, that perhaps it's not something that needs to be measured.

He looks at her, then continues:

Carl In class last week you spoke about rhyme. How in English, because there aren't so many words that rhyme, when one does it's to show off – your mind, your cleverness. Whereas in French, with so many, you rhyme as the heart pumps, as you breathe, as the eyes blink.

Claudie I must be a better teacher than I thought, none of you seemed to be –

Carl I don't know what you mean. It doesn't make sense to me. (*Recites.*)
'Oui, puisque je retrouve un ami si fidèle,
Ma fortune va prendre une face nouvelle.'
(*Explains.*) The opening of *Andromaque*.

Claudie Yes. (*She smiles.*)

Carl I learned it so I could speak as one breathes, as one's eyes open and shut. (*Continues.*)
'Et déjà son courroux semble s'être adouci
Depuis qu'elle a pris soin de nous rejoindre ici.'

Claudie Good for you, Carl. You should recite for the class –

Carl No. You talked about reading Proust? I've never read a word he's written.

Claudie You're young. You will.

Carl You said, Mme Melville, that to read Proust you must prepare as though for your honeymoon, when one knows that over a period of days two lifetimes will be for ever entwined, joined together, where passion spent only sows more passion and more nights together, and mornings, and long, grey afternoons.

Beat.

What does that mean? I really want to know what that means. Every day I notice things, Mme Melville. Every day I hear myself speak, think – I want to know. I write down notes, I imagine asking you.

Beat.

Claudie Ask me.

Carl *The Magic Flute.* What's it about? What does it sound like?

Claudie That's easy, I have the album here.

Then before she can look:

Carl William Faulkner.

Claudie Yes?

Carl I bought a book. I can't figure it –

Claudie Which one?

Carl I don't know how to pronounce it. *Absalom –* (*He mispronounces it.*)

Claudie Let me loan you another. That's the hardest, I think.

Carl (*on to the next*) The painting in your hallway. The woman in the bathtub.

Claudie The print.

Carl (*over this*) Whose is it?

Claudie (*going to the bookcase*) Pierre Bonnard. I have a book.

She finds the book.

Carl You said in class one day that you'd been an actress –

Claudie For only a year, years a—

Carl And singer. (*She brings the book back and sets it down.*) And just before Easter you sang a song. What was that song?

Claudie It was just before Lent. And we'd had wine in the faculty lunchroom –

Carl What is the song, Claudie?

His saying her first name stops her.

I'm sorry I –

Claudie No. Don't be sorry. I like my name.

Claudie hesitates, then quietly sings a short bit of an Edith Piaf song. She suddenly stops, turns and rubs Carl's hair.

I think the Opera House will be doing *The Magic Flute*. Let me take you.

Carl (*on to another question*) In the toilet – on the walls. You did that? It's a collage?

Claudie Yes, I suppose so. It's –

Carl From books. Postcards. Magazines. You did that?

Claudie I did.

Carl Of naked men and women.

Claudie Mostly.

Carl And words. You also cut out of –

Claudie It's supposed to be – fun. Funny. Something to look at in the toilet. Is that what kept you in there? The naked women – ?

Carl It's not important then.

Claudie No, it –

Carl I'm not missing something?

Claudie It is not – It's meaningless, Carl. It was done for – to be funny.

Carl (*having picked up the art book*) *Pierre Bonnard.* Is he important?

Claudie He is to me.

Carl Why?

Beat.

You don't know why?

Claudie I know why.

He looks at her.

Because there was a man – this was years and years ago – and he took me to a gallery. We first had lunch, then we passed the gallery where there was an exhibition of Bonnard. He took me in, we went from painting to painting. I remember each painting. I remember him holding with his hand my arm, and steering me from painting to painting, and asking me – what do I think? What does it make me feel? What do I see? (*She turns a few pages in the book.*) We went back out into the bright sunlight. It was June. Like now. We went to his apartment. And we made love. We then lived together for nearly three years.

They look at the book.

Carl Is this the book from that exhibition?

Claudie No. I didn't have money then to buy art books. I bought this later.

They turn pages, then:

Carl And if you hadn't gone with this man that day to this exhibition, you wouldn't think Bonnard important?

Claudie Probably not. Certainly not in the same way.

They look at one picture.

What do you see? (*She takes his arm.*) What does it make you feel?

He looks at her, then back at the picture.

Carl A woman after a bath. A nude woman.

Beat.

She is rubbing, cleaning her thigh with a cloth? One foot on a stool – no, it's a chair. She's wearing green shoes or slippers. She's looking down.

Claudie What makes you say she has taken a bath?

Carl Because the water's in the tub. She wouldn't let the water sit there and get cold. She'd get in.

She smiles.

What? Why is that funny – ?

Claudie Not funny. I think maybe I said almost the same thing to my teacher. We are two practical people, Carl. (*She squeezes his arm.*) And I think he smiled at me too.

Carl Your teacher? The man who took you to –

Claudie And he stood me in front of this very painting for a long long time before we spoke. 'Is she alone?' he

finally asked me. 'There's no one else in the picture,'
I answered. 'Or,' and he turned and looked at me,
'is someone watching her?' I hadn't thought of that.
'Is she aware that someone is – watching her? The
painter of this picture? Monsieur Bonnard? Perhaps,' he
continued, looking back at the painting, 'the bath has
been run for *him*. Perhaps,' he continued, now putting
his arm around my shoulder, (*She puts her arm around
Carl's shoulder.*) 'she has left their bedroom, walked
naked as we now see her, her green slippers clapping upon
the hard wood floor or whispering across the carpet, her
toes cracking as she passes their dishevelled bed and into
the hallway, and into – here. Her mission: to run *him* a
bath. And so now, as she waits, she cleans herself of their
lovemaking. Cleans off the "him" that got on to her. While
he, standing naked unseen in the doorway, watches.'

*Pause. They look at the painting. Her arm is still
around him.*

And then my teacher said, 'It may not be what Bonnard
intended, Mlle Melville. But it's what being here with
you has let me see.'

Short pause.

Twenty minutes later we're in his bed making love.

They look at the picture, then she turns the page.

(*About the next painting.*) With this I only see fruit in a
bowl on a table. Nothing else. (*Suddenly hears
something.*) Shh. (*Listens, then:*) I thought it might be
Ruth. She lives next – (*door*). (*She gestures.*) But it's
from upstairs. (*She takes his hand in hers and listens,
then, in a whisper:*) An old man lives up there. I think he
works in a publishing office. He's heavy and he walks
like – (*Mimics with heavy steps.*) But some days – nights
– one hears – (*Mimics light steps.*) Listen.

He tries to listen, but she now gently rubs his back.

A young woman, Carl? A young man? Definitely two different sets of steps. But I have never seen anyone but the gentleman on the stairs. (*Half to herself.*) You hear sounds – you can imagine all sorts of things. Things people are doing. (*Suddenly back to Ruth.*) Ruth's out on a – What time is it? She should be – (*Looks at Carl's watch.*) Oh God, look at the time! (*Suddenly stands.*) Carl, when's the last Metro?

Carl (*at the same time*) I think I've – (*missed it*).

Claudie (*at the same time*) You haven't missed the last Metro?

Carl It's too late.

Claudie (*over this*) How could we be so stupid!

Carl I'm sorry to make you drive me.

Claudie But I can't drive you.

Carl You offered – You said –

Claudie (*over some of this*) When did I – ? I wasn't thinking. My car's in the garage, Carl. I told you that. I told you that when we were waiting in line at the film.

Carl That's right. You did.

Beat.

I'll walk home then. (*He looks at Claudie.*)

Claudie You can't walk to the Sixteenth, Carl.

Carl Why not?

Claudie What about a taxi?

At first neither has an answer for this.

I'll phone your mother, she'll have to drive over and –

Carl She doesn't drive at all in Paris.

Claudie I think you told me that.

Beat.

And your father – won't be home yet?

Carl He's entertaining business friends. They could be out half the night.

Beat.

Claudie What do we do? (*Then the answer about the taxi.*) I don't have money for a taxi to –

Carl Neither do I.

Beat.

Claudie What are we going to do?

Beat.

Carl I don't know.

Claudie rubs her head.

Claudie I feel so stupid. I feel responsible –

Carl You're not responsible for me. I'm not a child.

She looks at him.

Claudie No. No, you are not. (*She smiles.*) There's the couch. You could stay here on the – It's not too comfortable. But what would your mother – ?

Carl I don't want to be any trouble.

Claudie It is my fault.

They look at each other. The entire previous 'conversation' has almost been spoken in quotes.

And you would be no trouble.

Carl I'll leave early. When the Metro –

Claudie Right after breakfast. First let me give you breakfast.

They look at each other, then:

Carl I'll call then . . . My mother.

Claudie looks at him, shrugs: 'What else can we do?'
Carl goes to the phone and dials.

(*Into the phone.*) Hello Mom? I've missed the last subway. We got talking and – That's a lot of money to waste on – Mme Melville's said I could stay on – their couch. I've said that. She says – Here, Mom, she wants to talk to you.

He holds out the phone. Claudie hadn't wanted to talk, but now has no choice.

Claudie (*clears her throat, sets down her wine glass, then*) Hello? Mrs – No. It is no bother at all. And it is all my fault. We got to talking about the film tonight and – Please.

Beat.

I don't mind, I assure you. Yes. I just don't know how I could be so stupid. Good. I will have him call the first thing. What? (*She gives Carl's mother her phone number.*) Medisee 4267. You're welcome. (*Starts to hang up, then:*) He's a very good student. You should be proud of him. Goodnight. (*Hangs up.*) She says it's fine. She doesn't mind.

Short pause. For a moment neither knows what to say, then:

Carl A lot of fifteen-year-old boys stay out until God knows when. And with God knows who. At least she knows I'm with my – teacher.

Claudie nods at this thought, suddenly hears footsteps upstairs.

Claudie Listen. The old man's got company. A girl or a boy? What do you think?

Beat.
As they listen:

Sometimes you also hear . . . noises. Let me get some sheets for the sofa.

She goes.

Carl She thinks you have a husband.

Claudie (*off*) What?

Returns with sheets. She looks at him.

Carl She thinks – there's a husband – (*Gestures: 'here'.*)

Beat.

My mother thinks – She asked the other day – if Mme Melville's husband went to the films with us.

Beat.

I think because of the 'Madame'.

Claudie starts to make the bed, Carl tries to help.

Claudie The school asked me to use –

Carl I know.

Claudie And what did you answer? About whether Mme Melville's husband went to the films?

Carl I said – he hasn't so far. I guess he doesn't like films.

She looks at him and smiles.

Claudie (*as they continue*) I don't have men's pyjamas . . .

Carl I don't need –

Claudie I keep a few new toothbrushes – I'll set one out.

Carl (*innocently*) Why do you keep new – (*Stops himself.*)

She watches him as they finish up the bed, pillows, etc. Then, as if out of the blue, to say something:

Claudie School's almost over. What are you doing for the vacation?

Carl My mother and I are going back to the States.

Claudie nods, lights a cigarette, offers one to Carl, who shakes his head, and they continue with the couch, etc.

Claudie (*getting the cigarette*) Whereabouts in the States – ?

Carl Ohio.

Claudie Where's that?

Carl In the –

Claudie Never mind.

Beat.

You looking forward to that?

No response.

I'll miss you. It's late, we should both get to bed. You want to use the bathroom first?

He hesitates, then looks towards the toilet, she stops him.

I might have something you could wear.

Carl I don't need –

Claudie Let me see how –

She measures his shoulders.

Carl (*quietly*) I'm fine in my underwear.

He looks at her, then goes off to the bathroom. Pause. Claudie finishes the last little bit of bed-making, and starts to pick up the wine and glasses, then decides to pour herself another glass.
    We hear water running in the bathroom sink.
    She sits down on the couch, sips her drink. Her eye catches the Bonnard book, she picks it up and starts to look through it.
    Toilet flushes off, and Carl returns.

Carl It's all – (*yours*).

Claudie (*over the book*) I then had to write a paper. My boyfriend who was also my teacher – who had taken me to see – he assigned a paper on art. And I wrote about Bonnard. I described this painting just as he had described it to me.

She turns to Carl, puffs on her cigarette.

I got the paper back, Carl – and it was full of red marks. Where's your critics? Where's your research? Where's your thinking? This is supposed to be an essay not a sentimental journey! (*She smiles, bemused, shakes her head.*) 'Think for yourself,' he wrote, at the top.

She closes the book, Carl tries to smile.

Teachers, right? (*And she sighs.*) You are finished?

He nods.

Anything you need – ?

He shakes his head.

Then – goodnight.

Carl Goodnight.

She stops and goes right up to him, hesitates, then holds out her hand for him to shake.

Claudie Goodnight.

They shake hands and she goes off to the bathroom. He turns off the lights; light now pours from the hallway and bathroom. In the dark, Carl takes off his jeans and shirt and gets under the sheets on the sofa.
Immediately Claudie, still dressed, returns and picks up her wine glass.

('*Explaining.*') I didn't finish my wine.

She sips. He doesn't move. In the darkness, she sniffles, it is clear that she is trying not to cry. Carl doesn't know what to do, then:

Carl Are you okay?

Claudie Yes. (*She smiles.*) Yes. I am okay. (*She sighs.*) Tonight, I am so happy not to be alone. Thank you. (*She finishes her wine.*) Here. Give me your hand. Give me your palm. (*She sits on the couch and he gives her his hand. She tickles the palm with her finger.*) Do you know what this means? When someone does this to your palm?

Beat.

It means they want to have sex with you. (*She tickles again.*) Like this. So if Lucy ever . . . Now you'll know. There aren't enough hours in the day to teach everything in school. (*She starts to get up, stops, and suddenly holds out her palm.*)

Want to try it?

He is frozen. She gets up, rubs his head and leaves, but immediately returns with a robe.

Try this on. I think it should fit. Stand up and try it on.

Carl hesitates getting out of bed in his underwear, but does so, and stands, embarrassed as she holds up the robe. He takes it from her and puts it on. Claudie stands back and looks.

That's better. In case you have to, now you don't have to walk around here just in your underwear.

Carl (*softly*) Goodnight.

He stands and watches her.
Claudie has gone to the records and begun looking through. After a moment, he half sits up and watches her, then:

Claudie Will this (*music*) bother you? I don't want to keep you up.

Carl No. It won't bother me.

Claudie Sometimes music helps me get to sleep.

Beat.

Carl (*quietly*) Me too.

She puts on an album: more jazz – perhaps Wayne Shorter or Charlie Parker.
Claudie sits on the floor and listens. She moves to the music, closing her eyes.
She sips from her drink, as the music plays for a while. Suddenly she stands up, startling Carl.

Claudie (*standing*) I know something you would be interested in. You weren't asleep?

He shakes his head.

There's a book – Come on. Get up. (*She starts to pull him up.*)

Carl Where are we – ?

Claudie (*over this*) I want to show you this book. It's in my bedroom.

Carl What sort of –

Claudie (*over this*) Shh. (*referring to the music*) Listen to that. I love that. Don't you love that. You are sleeping in the robe, Carl? How funny you are. You are very funny. Please, do you wish to see this book or not?

Carl What – ?

Claudie It's an art book, Carl. (*Finishes her wine.*) Come on. (*She takes his arm and leads him off.*)

Carl (*heading off*) An art book?

They are off.
    The music continues to play. Carl returns, still in his robe, now holding the 'art' book – an illustrated Kama Sutra of Vatsyayana.
    As the jazz continues under him, he speaks to the audience.

This was the art book. (*Opens and reads.*) 'Man is divided into three classes, the hare man, the bull man and the horse man, according to the size of his lingam. Women also, according to the depth of her yoni, is either a female deer, a mare or a female elephant.'

Beat.

'There are thus three equal unions between persons of corresponding dimensions, and there are six unequal unions, when the dimensions do not correspond, or nine in all as the following table shows.' (*He holds up the book to show us the table. Reading again.*) 'Equal: Hare/Deer. Bull/Mare. Horse/Elephant. Unequal – '

Beat.

212

Well – you can read it for yourself. The book, I've since learned, is readily available. (*Closes the book and goes and turns off the music.*) Anyway, we got to looking at this book in her bedroom and at the artwork which she said had true historical and aesthetic interest.

Beat. Carl begins to dress. As he dresses, he continues.

We laid on her bed and looked through the book. On our stomachs. Then she said she *had* to brush *her* teeth and she returned naked and rolled me over on to my back and undid the cord of the robe which I had already tied in a knot by accident.

Beat.

She had a design which ran across the top of her walls – blue and white, a pattern of shapes. I stared at that, then I closed my eyes.

Beat.

I stopped breathing. Or that's what it felt like. I heard every sound. Felt every pump of my heart.

Beat.

She sat upon me. She put me into her. I dared not open my eyes. My arms I kept straight against and alongside my body.

Beat.

She moved and almost instantly it happened. When I felt it, I wanted to let her know so she could move and get off, but she didn't move. It's the one time I opened my eyes. And she was smiling at me.

Beat.

She moved off.

Beat.

I heard her running a bath. She called me.

Claudie (*off, calls*) Carl!

Beat.

Carl The bath, she said, was for me. She stood, foot on chair, cleaning herself. It was years later before I realised what she had been doing – what she was . . . giving to me: that Bonnard painting.

Beat.

She smiled when I came into the bathroom. She winked. And said I was very handsome.

Beat.

She never took off her small silver cross, and it swung across her breasts as she cleaned.

Beat.

In bed I laid on my stomach and tried to sleep. She put an arm over my back, a leg over my thigh, and I'm pretty sure she fell asleep this way. Holding me this way.

Beat.

Again it was years and years before the thought occurred to me that perhaps this is what I gave her – something . . . breathing to hold on to in the night.

Beat.

I watched the dawn break through her white curtains, and still did not move until I felt the light pull, tug, of her fingertips against my bare side, and I then allowed myself to be righted again upon my back, and again she put me inside of her, and it happened all again – quickly.

Beat.

This time I opened my eyes and watched her face in the morning light. Her chin. The curve of her nose. Her mouth. But I tried not to look at any other part of her nakedness. Odd as it sounds, I felt that perhaps I shouldn't. (*He beings to 'unmake' the couch.*) The first train was, I think, at around six. But I remembered that she had wanted to give me breakfast.

Beat.

But she forgot about that.

Beat.

I found a roll in the kitchen. I made coffee. I lost myself in her books and records. I tried to stay out of her way, expecting to hear at any moment, 'Carl, shouldn't you be going?'

Beat. Claudie, in a robe, crosses from the bedroom to the kitchen. She smiles at Carl.

But these words were never said. She never spoke them.

Carl turns up the music and begins looking through the record albums.
    Pause.
    Knock on the door. Claude hurries to answer it.
    She returns following Ruth, her neighbour –
American, thirty. She is dressed in messy clothes, her hair uncombed, no make-up, etc.

Claudie (*entering*) Where's –?

Ruth He's just left.

They kiss on the cheeks

I just left him at the corner.

Claudie How did it go? He's – (*Carl*)?

Ruth (*to Carl*) Hi.

Claudie (*over this*) So what's he like?

Carl (*to Ruth*) Hello.

Ruth You must be one of Claudie's students she's always talking about.

Carl Is she always talking about me?

Ruth (*to Claudie*) We're going to a club tonight. He knows a lot of people in clubs. Are these yours? (*Cigarettes.*) You don't smoke.

Claudie They're Carl's.

Ruth He sings too. And plays the guitar. (*To Carl, taking a cigarette.*) You don't mind?

Claudie (*over this*) Coffee? Carl, do you want coffee?

Carl holds up his cup – he has coffee.

(*Over this.*) Ruth's from America –

Ruth (*continuing, not listening*) I think Robert's the first real French man I've found interesting.

Claudie moves towards the kitchen.

I don't want coffee.

Claudie stops. Ruth gestures to Carl – for a light. He picks up matches and lights her cigarette as:

By the way – (*puff*) we heard voices last night in here. We were coming up the stairs. It was late. Was there any . . .? (*Then she realises that Carl is more than a student and turns to him.*) Oh.

Claudie I'll have one of those too. (*Goes to take a cigarette.*)

Ruth (*looking over Carl*) I'm sorry, I didn't catch your name.

Claudie Carl.

Ruth Carl. How do you do, Carl.

Claudie (*heading for the kitchen*) You're sure you don't want – (*coffee*). (*She is gone.*)

Ruth (*still looking over Carl*) I'm Ruth. I live next door.

Carl I know.

Ruth So you're not one of Claudie's little students.

Carl Actually – I am.

    Beat.

One of her little students.

Ruth At the American School –

Carl Yes. (*She stares at him.*) I'm in the tenth grade.

    Claudie returns, bowl of coffee in hand.

Ruth (*to Claudie*) He's in the tenth grade.

Claudie (*smiles, sips, then*) We went to see a film last night. A group of students and me. Poor Carl here missed the last train.

    Short pause, as they sip, smoke, look back at the album jackets.

Ruth Enjoy the film?

Claudie I did.

Carl It was about surfing –

Ruth (*over this*) So you missed the last Metro. Poor boy.

Claudie And so he had to stay here with me. I fixed up the sofa for him. Didn't I?

    Short pause. Ruth watches as Claudie looks to Carl.

Claudie Don't be embarrassed.

Carl I'm not embarrassed.

Claudie Ruth understands. Don't you?

Ruth Sure.

Claudie (*suddenly, to Ruth*) So tell me – what's he like?

Ruth He says I should get a bigger bed. (*Then getting 'into' herself and her problems.*) This from a man who says he normally sleeps on the floor – or on one of those thinny thin mattresses from the Orient? What are they called? He gets into my bed – but he is a big guy. How tall do you think Robert is?

Claudie I only saw him the one –

Ruth We didn't wake you? I mean – he did play me two of his songs at something like four in the morning. I'm saying – Robert, shh, sing in the morning. He says – (*French accent.*) 'I sing when I feel like singing.'

   Beat.

I've never seen a naked man strum a guitar before – you know: bouncing. It's an unnatural sight. He's got a cousin who has offered him a job. (*More random memories.*) And an uncle who's somehow in the government. They don't speak. He's been to America twice. Once to Florida with his parents when he was a boy. Then once to Manhattan where he bummed around for about three weeks, living off people he just met, sleeping – wherever. Once he slept under someone's sink that had a drip. In the middle of the night, he said, they turned on a light and there he was trying to fix the drip. He's very handy. You know my record player that's been broken for weeks? He almost got it to work. That's what he said – he almost fixed it. (*She seems lost in a thought for a moment, then, changing gears, to Claudie, about Carl:*) He's really young. (*To Carl.*) Where in America are you from?

Carl Ohio.

Ruth Ohio. Never been there. I've been to Orlando, Florida. I've been to pretty much all of the East Coast states except for Maine and, I think, Rhode Island. I don't think I've been there. I'm from Montclair, New Jersey, do you know it? And New Hampshire. I haven't been there.

Carl No. I don't know it.

Ruth I tell people here that I'm from New York – same thing. But since you're an American –

Claudie Ruth's been taking classes at the Sorbonne, Carl.

Ruth Among other things. But not officially. But maybe that'll happen. I'm – I just sort of follow the crowds in and sit and listen to – whatever they happen to be teaching that day. You wouldn't believe some of the courses I've been sitting in on – they're all over the map. It's how I met Robert – I was on my way to one of these classes and he was playing his guitar and singing on the Rue des Ecoles. Right around the corner from – (*Gestures.*)

The phone rings. Claudie goes to answer it.

Claudie (*into phone*) Hello? Oh yes. He is. Just a minute. (*Covers phone.*) Carl. It is your father. He has to come into town this morning. He can pick you up.

Holds out phone. Carl hesitates.

Carl I can take the train, he doesn't have to –

Claudie Carl.

Continues to hold out the phone to him. Then as he takes it, she half whispers to him:

I was thinking of going to Le Louvre today. Is that something you'd like to do with me?

He looks at her.

(*Nods to the phone.*) I don't know if it is all right with . . .

Carl (*into phone*) Dad? What? Yes, she told me. Actually – Mme Melville –

Ruth looks at Claudie and smiles as she mouths: 'Madame Melville.'

– is taking a group of students to Le Louvre this – (*Turns to her.*) – afternoon?

She nods.

She asked if I – It's fine, Dad. I'll take the train. Dad, she – Yes, he's coming too! Goodbye. Bye! (*He hangs up. Short pause.*)

Claudie I hope I didn't create a problem, Carl.

He shakes his head.

Le Louvre is one of the most important museums in the world.

Carl He knows that. It's fine. I can go.

Claudie Good.

Ruth (*who has been paying close attention*) Who's the 'he' he was referring –

Claudie My husband. Carl's parents are convinced for some reason that I have a husband. I learned this last night, when they allowed Carl to stay . . .

Beat.

I suppose the 'Madame'. Which I use only for school.

No one knows what to say for a moment, then:

Carl He doesn't go to museums himself. They – scare him I think. My father. He doesn't like a lot of things. He doesn't like anything he doesn't understand.

Short pause.

Ruth So you two are going to Le Louvre today. With a group like you – ?

Claudie No. Just the two of us.

Beat.

Ruth I'd come too, but . . .

Claudie But what?

Ruth But you don't want me, do you?

Claudie (*smiling*) No.

Ruth And – what's the time? (*She takes Carl's wrist and looks.*) Jesus, I have a lesson in a minute.

Carl (*to Claudie*) Lesson?

Ruth Maybe I should have some coffee, if it's no –

Claudie (*on her way to the kitchen*) I'm getting it.

She is gone. Ruth sighs.

Ruth (*looking at herself*) These are the clothes I – I almost said that I slept in – but that isn't true. (*Smiles.*) That I wore last night. Just threw them on to go out for breakfast.

Claudie returns with coffee.

(*To Claudie.*) I paid for breakfast by the way. My ex-husband would never have let me do that. He'd have broken my arm if I tried to do –

Claudie (*to Carl*) Ruth was married back in –

Ruth Montclair.

Claudie How old is Robert? He looked like he could be –

Ruth Twenty-five? Twenty-eight? Nineteen? I don't know. (*To Carl.*) He's not in the third grade so you wouldn't know him.

Claudie smiles at the joke, Carl doesn't.

(*To Claudie.*) Since you brought him up –

Claudie Who? Robert or your ex – ?

Ruth (*over this*) What do I say about my ex-husband all the time?

Claudie I don't know. So you're talking about your ex – ?

Ruth About both of them. (*Turns to Carl.*) Carl, when we were in school, my ex and me – he was on the track team. And he wore those cute shorts that were really shiny, like fake-silky? You know what I –

Carl They still do.

Ruth He knows them. If it weren't for those shorts!

Sits back, sips her coffee, others wait, then:

(*To Claudie.*) I've told you this?

Claudie nods.

(*Referring to Carl.*) Will he mind if I –?

Claudie No. He won't.

222

Ruth (*to both of them*) I'm maybe eighteen and I accidentally touch with my hand those shorts. We're talking. Then we're – kissing and I touch.

Beat.

I lost my virginity against those shorts. I lost about eight years of my life because of those shorts. But the point I'm getting to, Claudie, is guess what kind of underwear Robert's wearing?

Claudie Fake-silky?

Ruth I didn't believe it. (*To Carl.*) You don't wear fake – ?

Claudie (*answering for him*) No. No, he doesn't.

Ruth Oh. Anyway – so why did I bring this up?

No response. She can't remember, but continues.

So they're silky, but they are also not too clean, I noticed. You don't think he has any – disease or anything? They really weren't clean. (*Lost in thought for a moment, then:*) Anyway. Thanks for the coffee. (*She gets up, takes Carl's wrist again and looks at his watch.*) They're probably waiting outside my door.

Claudie (*to Carl*) Ruth teaches violin.

Ruth (*kissing Claudie*) Have a nice time at Le Louvre. (*To Carl.*) Nice to meet you. (*Whispers to Claudie.*) He's so sweet. (*She goes, then immediately returns.*) They are outside my door. The mother and the student. (*She goes again. Short pause.*)

Claudie That's my neighbour, Ruth.

Beat.

She's American. (*She rubs his shoulders as he continues to look through albums.*) Like you.

She hugs him from behind. From off (Ruth's apartment), the sound of a child's violin lesson: start and stop as he/she plays the waltz 'Over the Waves'.

She's also a very fine player herself. (*Leans over him and points to the albums.*) Keep turning. A few more. There. Take that one out.

He takes out an album.

That's her. (*Points to a photo.*) That's her all-girl quartet. It's the only album they've made so far. But they're great.

He looks at the album. Child's lesson continues off.

Carl She didn't act like a . . .

Claudie Like a what?

Carl I don't know. I've never met a musician before.

Claudie They're not all like –

Carl I didn't think –

Claudie But they also don't walk around in black suits and ties and –

Carl I know that.

Claudie Good. I should get dressed. (*She doesn't get up, she reaches and holds back his hair off his face, rubs his head.*) Am I hurting you?

Beat.

I don't wish to hurt you.

She presses her face against the top of his head, sighs, then stands and goes to get dressed.
Pause. The music lesson continues. Also, slowly, the sounds of the outside begin to be heard – cars, life, street noise.

Carl speaks to the audience.

Carl That day we walked the halls and galleries of Le
Louvre for six hours, occasionally resting on a bench,
but always in sight of paintings to look at. The greatest
paintings, she would say, that the hand of man had ever
created.

Beat.
*The music lesson begins to fade. Over the course
of the speech, outside noise is replaced with echoing
inside-the-museum noise – coughs echoing, whispers
echoing, footsteps echoing.*
*Then they are replaced again by the sounds of
outside, along the Seine: traffic, boats, birds, children,
etc.*

She had walked these halls many many times before –
she had favourites over which she enthused, demanding
my enthusiasm. She had loves and she had hates, and she
had confusions.

Beat.

She spoke with two paintings as if they were old friends
– or to the people portrayed. I didn't know. She stopped
to let me hear the echoing voices, and steps.

He listens.
*Claudie appears in the bedroom doorway, finishing
getting dressed.*

Claudie Never close your ears, Carl. The greatest
mistake people make looking at art is to close their other
senses. But paintings live in sound. They live among
these footfalls, that child's cry. That man's cough. Those
sweethearts' whispers.

Beat.

Carl (*continuing to the audience*) She took me to a room she said she hadn't visited since she was sixteen. It's known, she said, as a great place where boys can pick up girls. Along one wall was an Ingres, his huge portrait called *Odalisque*. A young naked woman has her back to us, she is turning, lying, looking sensually at us. Her skin the colour – and the taste, she insisted – of honey.

Beat.

Girls came here, she explained –

Claudie (*in the doorway, putting on her shoes*) – because after the boys looked at this Ingres, every girl's ass looks inviting. (*Claudie disappears back into her bedroom.*)

Carl Two teenage girls sat on a side bench, hands folded in their laps, giggling. When I turned to look at them, they stopped and stared down. I felt Mme Melville stick her finger in my back pocket and pull me away – jealously, I think. (*He smiles.*) Then as we moved, I felt her finger stroke back and forth across my butt, inside my pocket.

Beat.

Not every painting or sculpture in Le Louvre is of a nude. But nearly every one, or perhaps every one, is – of a body. Mme Melville's words.

Beat.

You take away the body, its muscles, its flesh, its sex –

Claudie (*coming out of the bedroom*) – and you empty this building. (*Fixing her stockings, brushing her hair, etc., as she prepares to go out.*) Carl, a man is not only his sex . . .

Carl She said this as we stared at a painting of a very healthy-looking saint with arrows sticking though his muscular torso –

Claudie (*continuing*) But a man's sex is what makes him a man.

Beat.

Carl I said to her: 'No one ever put it that way in Ohio.'

As Claudie continues to get ready behind him.

One painting confused me. I remember its name – I bought a postcard of it years later. *Gabrielle d'Estrées and Her Sister.*

Beat.

Two young women are shown naked from the waist up – there's a sort of curtain covering below that. One – Gabrielle or her sister? – has reached over with her hand and is pinching or holding the other's naked nipple. Both look at the artist. At us. What is this about? I asked Mme Melville and she explained –

Claudie The world's a lot more interesting than we give it credit for. (*She disappears into her room.*)

Carl Outside we walked together along the Quai du Louvre. Mme Melville stopped at a kiosk and purchased a small book of paintings from the museum. I watched her take out her money, bending a leg to hold up the purse. The late-afternoon, early summer's sun seemed to touch her and set her apart from the world. As if a sculpture. As if a work of art.

Beat.

I felt more desire than I'd ever in my life felt before.

Beat.

The book was for me. She brushed back her hair, which the wind off the Seine kept blowing across her face. 'A souvenir,' she explained, as she placed it into my jacket pocket. The expression on my face, I think, stopped her, stopped her smiling. And then for the first time, though we had been together all day, all night, in her apartment, in her bed, I reached and I touched her. I touched her arm, and then held it. And I would have kissed her – until then I had never kissed a girl – but I would have kissed her had she not suddenly run off.

Short pause.

She ran to a man I recognised as Monsieur Darc, my mathematics teacher at school. With him was his young daughter holding a balloon. They kissed each other on the cheeks. They spoke. She seemed to talk very sternly at him. They did not kiss goodbye.

Beat.

Walking home she asked if I wanted to stop for coffee. Then she ordered wine. Suddenly it was like I wasn't even there. She found a pair of sunglasses in her bag and put them on. We sat there for a long time. And then we returned to her apartment.

Carl goes to the doorway, and returns with Claudie, as they enter from their outing to Le Louvre.
Silence. No one speaks.
Carl takes out his new book from his jacket pocket. Claudie remains distracted.

(*Holding the book.*) Thank you for the –

Claudie Put some music on, will you?

He hesitates.

What are you looking at? What are you looking at?

Carl (*confused at her outburst*) What kind of music do you –?

228

Claudie I don't care! Something! (*She takes off her shoes, and heads for her bedroom. As she goes, she mumbles under her breath:*) Men.

She is gone. He puts music on. Ruth has entered, she has changed – looks great, well dressed, hair fixed, etc.

Ruth I heard you come in. Is Claudie – ?

He turns towards the bedroom. As Ruth heads for the bedroom:

Can you turn that (*music*) down?

He turns it down as Claudie comes out, putting on a sweater.

(*Explaining.*) I heard you come in –

Claudie (*going to Carl*) Why can't you keep that out of your face? (*A bit aggressively, she pushes back his hair.*) And I can't hear that.

He turns the music up.

Ruth How was Le – ?

Carl It was great.

Claudie (*over this*) I ran into Paul. And I'm sick and tired of running into Paul. Every day at school I have to run into Paul! There he is with a big smile on his face like nothing has happened! Buying his daughter balloons! (*Seeing Carl.*) I'm sorry. Carl, you should get home.

Carl Why?

Claudie Why? Because it is time you went home.

Ruth By the way, your mother stopped by, Carl.

Carl My mother?

Ruth She said she was your –

Claudie (*over this*) Did you give your mother my address?

Carl No. I –

Claudie How did she get my address then, Carl?

Ruth She said she called the school.

Claudie It's Saturday. No one's at the school.

Ruth I think she said she got the address from the headmaster at school. So I assumed she had called the –

Claudie She called the headmaster at his home.

Ruth She said she was just in the neighbourhood. I told her you'd probably be back . . . (*Takes Carl's wrist and looks at his watch.*) Soon.

Pause. No one knows what to do.

(*Noticing.*) You have my album out. Have you been playing – ?

Claudie Not yet.

Beat.

Carl wants to hear it.

Pause. The music continues to play.

Ruth (*standing*) I think I'm in the way – I'm sorry.

She heads off. In the hallway, Ruth bursts out crying.

Claudie Ruth? Why are you crying? (*She follows her off. Off.*) Are you all right?

Carl sits and doesn't know what to do. Off, Claudie tries to get Ruth to talk:

What is it? Ruth? Tell me.

Then mumbled talk, and Claudie leads Ruth back into the room and immediately out into the kitchen.

Carl (*as they pass*) What's – ?

They are gone.

Is there anything I can do?

Pause. Music plays. Claudie returns, crosses the room and exits towards the bathroom.

What can I – ?

She is gone. She returns holding a bottle of white liquid.

Claudie (*as she heads back to the kitchen*) She has crabs. (*She stops.*) Robert, the naked bouncing guitar player, gave her crabs. (*She starts to go, then stops.*) You know what crabs are, don't you?

He hesitates.

They're little –

Carl Sure.

She looks at him and goes. A moment later Ruth comes out, followed by Claudie holding the bottle.

Ruth (*entering*) I'll take a shower in a minute. I just got dressed. I don't feel like taking my clothes off yet. Where are those cigarettes?

Carl finds the cigarettes, she goes to get one.

(*To Carl.*) They're really disgusting. They look just like little . . .

He slightly moves away.

You don't get them by sitting next to someone, Carl. (*She laughs to herself, then quickly turns to Claudie, wiping the tears off her face.*) How come you have a bottle of stuff for . . . (*Points to the bottle.*)

Beat.

Never mind.

Carl (*to Ruth*) Is that (*music*) too loud?

Ruth What?! Why are French people so unclean?!

Short pause. Claudie is hurt. Ruth realises this. Sighs, then:

Why are men so unclean?

Ruth reaches out towards Claudie who comes and takes her hand and sits with her. Ruth sniffles. Short pause.

Claudie I remember when I had to get that stuff (*the crabs medicine*). You have to get a prescription first. Which I did. I took it to a pharmacy.

Ruth Why didn't *he* get the –

Claudie shrugs and continues.

Claudie I stand in line. I hand the paper to the pharmacist and he says in a loud voice: 'What is this for?'

Beat.

'Crabs,' I half mumble. (*In a loud voice.*) 'Crabs!' he repeats back. Then the woman behind me. She's about – (*To Carl.*) Probably your mother's age.

Ruth (*trying to joke*) Which is what – your age?

Claudie smiles.

Carl (*joining the joke*) No, Mom's a little younger.

Ruth laughs hard at this.

Claudie She taps me on the shoulder and says, though
it says on the bottle to shower twice a day with it, she'd
found three times was really needed especially for the
men. Because of all the folds and things. I'm serious.
Then she stands and sort of mimes a penis – we're in
the pharmacy – in line. Stands there – (*Claudie mimes
this.*) And she says you have to really check all around it.
Lift it up. Look here, there. She said either I should help
or he should get his mother.

*Laughter. The phone rings. Claudie goes and picks it
up, listens for an instant, then:*

(*Into phone.*) Who? I'm sorry. (*She hangs up, goes back
and sits down. To Carl.*) It was your father.

Short pause. Music plays.

(*To Ruth.*) So he gave you crabs.

Beat.

Ruth So you ran into Paul.

Carl Is 'Paul' Monsieur Darc?

Ruth That's right. She and Monsieur Darc had been
going out together.

Carl But Monsieur Darc is married.

Ruth (*picking up the book on the table*) What's this?
The *Kama Sutra*? I didn't know you had this.

Claudie I don't usually keep it out here. Are you going
out with Robert tonight?

She ignores the question.

Then you'll eat with us. Carl and I haven't eaten all day.

Carl Am I staying for – ?

233

Ruth (*suddenly standing*) Carl wants to hear my album. Let's put it on for him! (*Leans over Carl and rubs his head.*) You little music lover, you.

Claudie Ruth, please.

Ruth (*surprised*) I wasn't . . .

Carl has managed to put on the album: an early Beethoven or Mozart.

How was Le Louvre? Did you show him the pick-up room? Shh. That's me. Hear me?

They listen. Phone rings again. Claudie hesitates, then goes and answers it.

Claudie (*into phone*) Hello? Yes. One moment. (*Covers the receiver.*) It's your mother, Carl.

Carl stands and goes to the phone. Music plays.

Carl (*into phone*) Hello? Yes, I had a great time. Incredible art. (*Beat.*) What time is it now? (*Looks at his watch.*) Actually we all were about to start making dinner. The whole gang here. A French dinner. Monsieur Melville is supervising.

Claudie and Ruth start making background noise of a group of students together. Carl nods to them – 'louder'.

Sorry, Mom, I can't hear. (*To the room.*) Hey everyone could you keep it down?

They don't.

(*Into phone.*) What? Sorry. I have to go. Monsieur Melville needs my help with something! Bye!!

Hangs up. The others are quiet. Music plays. Silence.

Claudie Don't upset your parents, Carl. You shouldn't do that.

Phone rings again.

(*Into phone.*) Hello? (*Holds out phone.*) It's your father.

With music playing, Carl takes the phone.

Carl (*hesitates, then into phone*) Dad?

Carl says nothing. Shouting from the phone. He listens, then after a while, with the shouting continuing, he just hangs up. He sits back on the sofa. Claudie and Ruth don't know what to say.

Ruth (*referring to the music*) That's me too.

Beat.

(*Holding up the* Kama Sutra.) Can I borrow this sometime?

Carl (*to Claudie*) I want to stay here.

Claudie Think what you're doing.

Carl (*yells*) I know what I'm doing!

Claudie is taken aback by this outburst.

Claudie (*after a glance at Ruth, who still has her head in the book*) You're a wonderful boy. (*She reaches for his hand.*) We've had a lot of fun.

Beat.

You're more than a boy . . . but is it worth it, Carl?

Carl It is.

He refuses her hand. She looks at Ruth, who looks up and nods, as if to say, 'Tell him.'

Claudie You've been so – good to be with. I've enjoyed myself so much. Thank you.

Beat.

Ruth Claudie . . .

Claudie (*looks at Ruth, then*) Ruth is right. I should tell you.

Carl Tell me what?

Claudie Monsieur Darc and I – Monsieur Darc, your mathematics teacher, and I – we had an argument this week, Carl . . . An awful argument. And we agreed not to see each other – again. See each other – as we have been seeing each other, I mean. I was hurt by this. Very hurt, Carl. I needed someone. Last night I needed some . . . I don't love you.

The phone starts to ring.

Ruth (*referring to the music*) Maybe I should turn this – (*off*).

Claudie No.

She looks at Carl and starts to cry. Carl just looks at her, confused. Speaking over the ringing phone.

(*Sniffling.*) That's not totally true. What I've just said . . . I . . . (*Rubs her sniffling nose.*) I have hated myself today. Whenever I've allowed myself to think – what do you think you're doing, Claudie, he's . . . I have hated myself. Please go home.

No one moves. Carl stares at Claudie, then:

Carl I'm staying here.

Beat. The phone stops ringing.

Ruth (*suddenly standing*) What about wine? We should have wine if we're having dinner.

Claudie (*wiping her eyes*) There are bottles in the –

Ruth I know where you keep it.

She goes off into the kitchen. Carl has watched her go.

Carl (*to say something*) Ruth looks so different. Than this morning. (*He hands her his handkerchief.*) In that dress. It's like she's another person. Like she's – beautiful. I suppose she is. Before I didn't think she was beautiful at all.

Claudie (*blowing her nose now into the handkerchief*) Women change. And there is a lesson in life, young man, that you will learn something like one or two billion more times.

She smiles and winks at him and hands him back his handkerchief. Phone rings again. They let it ring. Claudie sighs, breathes deeply, and goes and turns up the music, then sits next to Carl on the sofa. The phone ringing stops.

What will he do to you?

He puts her hand on his leg. Ruth enters with a bottle of wine and a corkscrew.

Ruth Here's the wine. Now shouldn't we have our man here open it? It is a man's thing to do.

Claudie 'Please, sir – could you help us girls?'

He takes the bottle and starts to open it.

Ruth Look at those muscles, Claudie.

Claudie I'm looking.

Ruth Us girls couldn't do that.

Claudie (*pushing the joke*) No-o-o-o.

Cork pops.

Carl What shall it be, ladies? (*Holds up the bottle.*) Red or – (*Picks up the crabs medicine.*) – white?

The women are disgusted.

Ruth For a minute there I forgot he was thirteen.

Claudie (*'correcting' her*) Twelve.

He pours. Music plays. Ruth pauses as she hears herself play.

Did you call Robert and tell him about the crabs?

Ruth Why would I – ?

Beat.

I did. And he knew. He's known.

The music ends and there is applause on the record. Claudie and then Carl join in the applause.

It's the only record we've made so far. The only piece. The rest of the album's other groups –

Claudie (*to Carl*) I was there. I was in that audience. (*Listening to the applause.*) There – that's me.

Ruth (*getting the joke*) Shut up. (*She smiles.*)

Applause on the record ends. Claudie goes to turn it off.

Carl Can we play it again?

Claudie starts it again.

Ruth It was quite a night, wasn't it? Everything I'd dreamed of in my clean kitchen in Montclair, New Jersey.

The music continues: they listen.

Claudie I'd never seen an all-girl string quartet before. It seemed really strange, you know. Good but strange. Like – I don't know.

Ruth (*picking up the album cover*) Hélène is the real beauty. Beautiful red hair. That's red hair (*photo in black and white*). The cellist.

Carl looks at the photo.

Claudie Carl was saying he thinks you're beautiful, Ruth.

Carl is embarrassed.

Carl Why did you – ?

Ruth (*at the same time*) When did – ?

Claudie (*continuing*) When you were – (*Gestures.*) How you look now. Isn't that right?

He says nothing.

Ruth You've put him on the spot.

Claudie (*back to the concert*) I went with Paul. (*To Carl.*) Monsieur Darc. And his wife. As sort of a teachers' group. And he said he had never even seen a female cellist before. (*To Carl.*) They're hardly in orchestras.

Ruth Women.

Claudie You never see them. (*Back to Ruth.*) And just watching Hélène play, with her thighs, Paul said, wrapped around it – it was, he said, one of the most sensual things he'd ever seen. Or heard.

Beat.

He said this to both me and his wife.

Ruth When I left Montclair and my husband and my baby –

Carl turns on hearing this.

Claudie (*explaining*) She left her baby.

Ruth (*explaining more*) My mother-in-law convinced me she'd be a better mother. (*Continuing her story.*) My husband laughed in my face. Going to Paris? For Christ's sake, girl, what do you want? I said what I wanted is . . .

Beat.

I'm sure I said something stupid. Something I'd heard. Something I don't believe in any more. Because I suppose I didn't know.

Beat.

But then came that night. (*Gestures towards the album. Pause.*)

Carl (*getting it, to Claudie*) That's when she knew why she –

Claudie I understood.

Beat.

He beat her, Carl.

Ruth I hit him too. Sometimes I hit him first. I don't blame him for that. I didn't leave for that. Let's not hear any more.

Claudie picks up the needle again and sets it on the end of Ruth's 'cut'. So we hear only the applause again. They listen to the applause until it ends, drink their wine. Ruth has picked up the Kama Sutra *again.*
When the applause ends, Claudie begins to put on more music. As she does:

Claudie I'd never let a man hit me.

Ruth (*taking a cigarette from the pack*) Cigarette?

Claudie Please. (*Hands her one.*)

Carl I'd love to come and hear you play.

Claudie Carl has been learning about music. His family doesn't listen to music. So he's practically a virgin.

   Beat.

Practically.

   Beat.

I've promised to take him to *The Magic Flute*.

Ruth When I was about your age – How old is he?

Claudie Fifteen.

Ruth I was fourteen. I got – I asked for and I got a recording of *The Magic Flute* for Christmas.

Carl How did you know even to ask for – ?

Ruth I just did. (*Continuing.*) I played it over and over in my room. On my little portable plastic record player.

   Claudie nods. She knows the type.

My friends, they were only interested in – (*Shrugs.*) Elvis Presley? I don't know. In all sorts of things I wasn't interested in at all. That I thought were stupid. That I still think are stupid. My ex – he loved that stuff. He made me dance to it with him. The son of a bitch even laughed at me when I practised. What's that going to get you? What is that – *about*? I felt like a freak in that house. And maybe I was. I'll play for you sometime. (*Smiles at Carl.*)

Carl Thank you.

Claudie Robert, I thought, plays the guitar and . . .

Ruth I wasn't interested in his guitar playing.

They laugh, calm down, then quietly:

Robert and his little tiny friends (*his crabs*). Look at this. I was looking through this (*the* Kama Sutra). There's – (*Finds the reference.*) – 'the widely opened position'. That's me. Completely open.

Claudie I don't think I've read any of the text. I bought it for the pictures. (*Looks at the book.*)

Ruth (*reads*) 'The yawning position.' That's me with my ex. 'The position of the wife of Indra.'

Claudie What is that one? The wife one.

Ruth (*reads*) 'When she places her thighs with her legs doubled on them upon her sides and thus engages in congress.'

Beat.

'This is learnt only by practice.'

Beat.

Claudie Jesus.

Ruth (*continues reading*) 'When a woman forcibly holds in her yoni the lingam after it is in, it is called the 'mare's position'. This too is learnt by practice only and is chiefly found among the women of the Andra country.'

Claudie (*turning to Carl*) Are you staying the night or . . .?

Carl I don't know.

Ruth (*reads*) 'When a man supports himself against a wall, and the woman, sitting on his hands joined together and held underneath her, throws her arms around his neck, and putting her thighs alongside his waist, moves herself by her feet, which are touching the wall against which the man is leaning, it is called the "suspended congress".'

Beat.

Claudie (*unable to visualise this*) What??

Ruth hands her the book, pointing at the page.

Claudie There's no picture?

Ruth Not for that one.

Carl sits uncomfortably between them.

Claudie (*reads to herself*) 'When a man . . . against a wall –' Carl, come over to the wall.

Stands, pulling up Carl. He hesitates. He follows her, she reads:

'Against a wall.' (*She positions Carl against the wall.*) 'Woman, sitting on his hands . . .' (*As she joins his hands together.*) Like this. (*Reads.*) 'Underneath her.' (*She starts to climb up on to his hands.*) Pick me up. Carl. That's right. 'Arms around the neck –' Ruth, could you hold the book?

Ruth takes the book.

'Thighs alongside his waist.' (*To Ruth.*) Like this you think?

Ruth holds out the book for Claudie to read as she starts to climb on to Carl, whose back is pressed against the wall.

'Moves herself by her feet.' (*She is on him, starts to move her feet.*) Is that right? Did I skip something?

She looks to Ruth, moves her feet. Carl is trying to keep his balance.

(*To Carl.*) Keep holding. (*To Ruth.*) What does that – ?
(*To Carl.*) Carl, you're letting me – Carl!

> *They stumble away from the wall. Claudie calls to
> Ruth for help, she tries to push him back to the wall,
> until finally, as Claudie screams, Carl and she fall,
> laughing.*
> *Carl takes this chance quickly to kiss her – the first
> time he has.*
> *She realises this and kisses him back.*

Claudie (*not a question*) You are staying tonight.

Ruth I think I should go. I –

Claudie No, no, not yet. Please, we were going to eat.
What happened to eating?

Ruth I don't think anyone's hungry. I'm not hungry.

Claudie You should eat. Remember you're eating for
more than one now.

Ruth Christ.

Carl (*not understanding*) What, is Ruth – ?

Claudie For five or six hundred or more now.

> *Carl realises that it's another joke about the crabs.*

Then let's at least open another bottle of wine. Drink up.

Carl (*the wine bottle is still half full*) We haven't
finished –

Claudie We will! I'll get the wine!

> *Claudie goes to the kitchen. Music plays.*
> *Ruth and Carl say nothing for a moment, but they
> smile at each other.*

Ruth (*finally*) That – (*Carl against the wall*) was funny.

Carl nods.
  Short pause, then:

Carl (*as if explaining everything*) She's my teacher.

Beat.
  They burst out laughing.
  Beat.

Ruth Claudie was telling me about a student of hers who was going to be a poet.

This stops him.

So that's you.

Beat.

You don't have any of your poems – ?

Carl I don't know what I'll be.

Ruth Claudie has tons of poetry books.

Carl I know. I've seen.

Claudie (*entering with wine and cheese*) Where's our man (*to open the wine*)?

Ruth Claudie should show you her writing.

Claudie (*protesting*) Ruth, I'm not going to show –

Ruth (*to Carl*) She's writing a novel.

Carl You never said –

Claudie (*over this*) What literature teacher hasn't tried to write a novel? Choose some music.

Ruth Show him. He'd be interested –

Claudie Carl, you choose –

Carl I don't know what to –

Ruth (*over this*) You want to know what it's about? It's about –

Claudie Don't tell him! (*Covers his ears.*) It sounds stupid talking about it.

Beat.

Ruth It's interesting.

Carl I'm sure it –

Claudie (*trying to change the subject and make a joke*) Open the wine, young man. Earn your keep. Make up for your inability to perform – the suspended congress or whatever it was called in the book?

No response. Carl and Ruth just look at her.

(*To Ruth.*) Why did you bring that up?

Ruth (*to Carl*) I'll choose some music.

She takes the job away from a reluctant Carl. She will put something quiet on – piano music.
Pause.

Claudie (*finally*) Okay. Every student should get at least once the chance to laugh at his teacher. (*She heads off to her bedroom.*)

Carl I won't laugh.

The music is on. Claudie returns with a box of papers and sets them down. Carl has just opened the bottle of wine.

Claudie (*holding out her glass to Carl*) I need a drink for this.

He pours.

It takes place, of course, in the Middle Ages.

Carl Why 'of course'?

Ruth Because it's about –

Claudie Shh.

Beat.

Ruth She's done a lot of research and –

Claudie Ruth.

Beat.

A specific period: November 1429 to about the next
March, 1430. Four and a half months. Mostly in a large
barn, it's actually a workshop attached to a convent –
outside Paris. A group of women, mostly nuns – but
nuns at this time, it's complicated. Here is where they
paint. You've seen – I showed you a couple today, Carl –
the manuscripts painted called illuminated manuscripts.
Did you know that many of these – all of which are
attributed to monks, to this monastery or that order
of monks – were in truth painted by women?

Beat.

Sort of 'farmed out' art. To different convents – who
got no credit but a little money from the monks – who
got a lot more from – whomever was paying.

Beat.

So some of the nuns here – well, their major skill was
painting and so pretty much anyone could be a nun if
they painted well – that was *the* qualification – so you
could in fact *be* other things. You couldn't be married,
but you could have men. You could have children. But
you were a nun.

Beat.

Into this barn, one day, comes a man in a suit of armour.
A short man. Visor down, staggering under the weight of
the metal. The women, seeing the soldier and fearing the
worst, try and flee, but a voice calls out from inside the
armour:

'Stop. Please. I'm not here to hurt you.'

And the soldier falls to the dirt ground. One of the
women goes to him, hesitantly, and in removing the
helmet realises – the man is a woman.

Ruth The most famous woman –

Claudie Jeanne d'Arc.

Beat.

Let me backtrack for a second. By the autumn of 1429,
Jeanne d'Arc was without doubt the most famous
woman in France – in the world maybe, but certainly
in France. She'd helped us capture Orléans, and helped
crown the Dauphin. Because of this her movements are
well documented – part of history. A day-by-day account
of what she did, where she was – can be put together.
(*She sips, then:*) Until November 1429. And for the next
four months. With the sole exception of a single visit to
Orléans where she was seen by others only at a distance,
and from a balcony. Except for this – Jeanne's
whereabouts are unknown. As are the reasons for her
disappearance. All this is true.

Beat.

So it is Jeanne d'Arc on this dirt ground, in the convent's
barn. And why is she here, Carl? Because – she's pregnant.

*Phone rings. They hesitate, then Claudie nods to
Ruth, who gets up and gets it.*

Ruth (*into phone*) Hello? It's Ruth. (*She turns to
Claudie.*) It's Paul.

Carl is relieved, thinking of course it was his father.

Claudie I'm busy.

Ruth looks at her.

I am busy.

Ruth (*into phone*) She's busy. (*Hangs up.*)

Claudie (*after another drink, then*) The Maid of Orléans, the virgin princess, this woman whose very purity is the definition of France – has fallen.

Beat.

She is taken in. Allowed to sleep in the hay. She grows larger. For a long time she won't speak. The women, one day, get her to pose, naked, pregnant, for a painting of the Virgin Mary. They needed a model.

Beat.

She will say nothing of the father. She is still obsessed with her own purity. 'What does that –' her bulging stomach – asks one of the women, 'have to do with purity?' This particular woman was a very fine painter and a nun in name only.

Beat.

Finally – and I'm skipping way ahead now – the Dauphin's people find her. That's when she has to go to Orléans and hide behind the railing on the balcony.

Beat.

The Dauphin's people are shocked. They predict the fall of France. Scholars are brought in and there is a movement to declare it an immaculate conception and the Child of God. The brother – or sister – of Jesus. The men debated this and the debate takes two months.

Meanwhile Jeanne is allowed to return to the barn and the nuns. And there, in March 1430, she gives birth, with profound pain, to a baby girl.

Short pause.

The next day she puts her armour back on and returns to the Dauphin's side, where she stayed, until being captured and burnt at the stake.

Beat.

It's a story about a lot of things, but mostly I think it's about a woman who risks everything to have a child she knows she doesn't want.

Beat.

I've been pregnant three times. But I have no child.

Pause.

(*Quietly.*) The last was your mathematics teacher's. (*She fiddles with the pages of the manuscript.*) It's not finished. (*She closes the box top and suddenly to change the subject and mood she grabs the* Kama Sutra, *quickly finds a page and reads.*) 'When after congress has begun the woman places one of her legs on her lover's shoulder and stretches the other out –'

Carl starts to open the box of papers.

Claudie Don't read it.

Carl closes the top. Ruth who is still by the albums suddenly holds one up:

Ruth (*showing Claudie*) Claudie?

Claudie (*smiling*) Why not? He knows everything else about us.

Carl is curious now.

Ruth (*to Carl*) You heard this? 'Les Djinns Singers.'

Carl No, who – ?

Ruth My brother gave this to me as a going-away present. He meant it as a joke, but we love it, don't we?

Claudie (*taking the album and reading the title*) 'Sixty French Girls Can't Be Wrong!'

As Claudie puts it on:

Carl Why is it – (*here*)?

Ruth My record player's been broken for –

Claudie (*reading the back of the album*) 'From Paris, come these sixty Princesses, to raise their voices in exuberant and sentimental song in a dozen varied selections.'

Ruth (*jumps up and reads*) 'What makes these renditions all the more outstanding is the fact that the entire assemblage consists of –'

Both '– jeune filles –'

Claudie '– between the ages of thirteen and sixteen!'

Ruth Your age, Carl!

Claudie 'Each youngster was especially auditioned and selected on the basis of personal qualification and aptitude, and after an – unusually exacting audition.' Bite your tongue, Ruth.

> *Claudie puts the needle down on the song 'Oui Oui Oui' – sung by these sixty jeune filles. It is silly and kitsch. As soon as the music starts or just a fraction before, Claudie and Ruth form a 'line' and mouth along. Doing a dance number they have worked out – obviously they have done this many times before.*

Carl watches, smiling. The women can barely keep a straight face.

(*As they dance.*) I think we've been alone together too many Saturday nights!

As the song plays, Carl has picked up the album to read it. Suddenly Claudie hurries to her bedroom.

(*Rushing off.*) I'll be right back. Right back.

Ruth I know what she's going to get.

As the song plays, Ruth opens a small drawer in a table and takes out a small bag of marijuana and some wrappers.

(*To Carl.*) Do you smoke grass?

Claudie runs out of her bedroom putting on white socks. She has another pair for Ruth.

Claudie (*explaining*) To make us – jeune – (*Sees what Ruth is doing, almost says something, then doesn't.*) Sixty-two French girls can't be wrong.

Ruth (*taking the socks*) I'm not French.

Claudie In spirit you are! (*Then she has to say something.*) He doesn't smoke dope.

Ruth How do you know? (*To Carl.*) You smoke dope?

Carl Sure.

Song continues. Ruth has put her white socks on and grabs Carl and dances with him. Claudie puts on her socks. As she does, she watches the two dance. Ruth starts to get quite close to Carl.

Claudie (*finally, after having seen enough*) Ruth, stop it. That's enough. (*To Carl.*) Come here.

Carl There is a poem I could read. I have a copy – It's in my –

He takes a piece of paper out of his pocket.

Claudie You have one of your poems with you, Carl? Why didn't you say –?

Carl (*reads*)
'Rhythms silent and –'

Claudie Wait, Carl.

She hurries and turns down the music.

Carl (*reads*)
'Rhythms silent and frail
Of delicate air
to catch the curling of hair.

'Voice crisp and curt,
O delicate voice,
Curling the catching air.

'Silent hands
catch the delicate rhythms
from the frail hair,
the silent and the frail hair.'

Beat.

Ruth (*turns to Claudie*) Is it about you?

Carl It's why I stayed back. Last night. In the toilet. To show it to you. So you might tell me what you think. There's more . . .

He hands her the poem.

Ruth I'll get my fiddle. I feel like playing. I'll be right back.

She goes.

253

Claudie (*while looking at the poem*) She doesn't play for everyone.

Carl I'm flattered. Let's put the *Sixty French Girls* back on –

Claudie I love the poem. Thank you. It was brave of you to show it to me.

She looks at him, smiles, pushes his hair back.

God, I wish I could cut this off.

She kisses him as Carl's father, a man in his forties, enters from the hallway. At first unseen. Then Carl turns and sees his father.

Carl (*in shock*) Father –

Father The door was open.

Claudie Monsieur –

Father Madame Melville. 'Madame' with no husband. I spoke with the headmaster.

The music plays.

Carl, let's go.

He doesn't move.

Let's go, Carl.

Ruth enters behind him with her violin. Then Father goes to Carl and with neither saying a word, he reaches around and picks Carl up around the waist and begins carrying him out like a child.

Carl, without words or sound, fights, kicks like a little boy having a tantrum. As they struggle, Carl kicks the sofa, kicks objects off a table.

The two women can barely look. Claudie suddenly tries to stop the music – and drags the needle over the record, scratching it.

*Now there is only silence and father and son
struggle. Only their breathing is heard, until finally,
after a great effort, Father carries his child off.*
   Pause.
   *Neither woman says anything. Ruth begins absent-
mindedly to pluck her violin strings.*
   *Lights shift and Carl returns and speaks to the
audience, as the women slowly fade away. He carries
a suit jacket.*

Carl I was taken out of the ironically named American
School immediately, and arrangements were made to
send me back to Ohio to live with my aunts.

   Beat.

I saw Mme Melville again only once. The night before
my departure, Father and Mother took me to a
restaurant for dinner. I requested something on the Left
Bank, near the Sorbonne. Father was suspicious. But
Mother, already upset that I was leaving, and missing me
terribly, agreed to whatever I wished.

   Beat.

We ordered. I went to wash my hands in the WC, and
kept running. I figured Father would know where I went,
but I also figured he wouldn't bring Mother with him,
nor could he leave her in the restaurant alone. This was
France after all. So he'd drive her home first and this
gave me time.

   Beat.

She wore a short, tight, black dress.

   *Claudie enters in a black dress, and turns and lets him
   zipper it up.*

I wore a suit that I thought made me look old.

   Claudie helps him on with his suit jacket.

When I arrived, she told me she had a date for that night, so I couldn't stay long. We sat together on the sofa. She put on music.

Claudie puts on an album.

What are you –?

Claudie *The Magic Flute.*

It is the 'Papageno–Papagena' duet. They listen. Claudie takes off her shoes and curls up next to him. He looks at her.

Carl (*about the music*) What are they – (*saying*)?

Claudie They love each other. They want to be together.

Beat.

Listen.

She touches him to get him focusing on a moment in the music.
They listen.
She touches his leg apparently by accident. He notices.

Excuse me.

She moves her hand. She looks up at him, then away.
Doorbell. He looks at her, then to the audience.

Carl (*to audience*) She asked me to stay until after she'd gone. She said she didn't want Paul, Monsieur Darc, my math teacher, to see me here.

Silence.
Claudie leans over and slips on her shoes. She stands and holds out her hand so Carl can steady her balance as she adjusts her shoes.

She looks at him, then turns and looks at the back of her skirt.

Claudie Is it smooth?

He nods.

No wrinkles?

He shakes his head.
She straightens the skirt anyway.
Slowly she walks towards the door. He watches her walk. She again runs her hand along her behind, to straighten out any wrinkles.
Carl continues to watch.
As she approaches the door, she turns back to him and, with only the tips of her fingers, she waves goodbye and is gone.
From the hallway we hear the door opening, a brief conversation, and the door closing.
The music goes out.
Pause.

Carl Years later. And years and years ago. When I was twenty-four, I ran into a friend from my Paris days. And he told me Mme Melville had died.

Beat.

Of cancer, he thought.

Pause.

(*To the air.*) May I see that good-bye one more time?

Beat.
Claudie returns (there is no sound of the door opening). She goes to the sofa and sits, taking off her shoes and placing them just where they were before.
She leans against Carl.

She leans over and slips on her shoes. She stands and holds out her hand so Carl can steady her balance as she adjusts her shoes.

She looks at him, then turns and looks at the back of her skirt.

Claudie Is it smooth?

He nods.

No wrinkles?

He shakes his head.

She straightens the skirt anyway.

Slowly she walks towards the door. He watches her walk. She again runs her hand along her behind, to straighten out any wrinkles.

Carl continues to watch.

As she approaches the door, she turns back to him and, with only the tips of her fingers, she waves goodbye and is gone.

From the hallway we hear the door opening, a brief conversation, and the door closing.

This time the music continues.

Pause.

End of play.